SAT Vocabulary Prep
Level 1

Other Kaplan Books for College-Bound Students

SAT Vocabulary Prep Level 2
SAT Premier Program
SAT Comprehensive Program
12 Practice Tests for the SAT
SAT Strategies for Super Busy Students
SAT 2400
SAT Critical Reading Workbook
SAT Math Workbook
SAT Writing Workbook
SAT in a Box
Warcraft Vol.1: A Kaplan SAT/ACT Vocabulary-Building Manga
Psy-Comm Vol. 1: A Kaplan SAT/ACT Vocabulary-Building Manga
Van Von Hunter Vol. 1: A Kaplan SAT/ACT Vocabulary-Building Manga
The Ring of McAllister: A Score-Raising Mystery Featuring
1,046 Must-Know SAT Vocabulary Words
Frankenstein: A Kaplan SAT Score-Raising Classic
The Tales of Edgar Allan Poe: A Kaplan SAT Score-Raising Classic
Dr. Jekyll and Mr. Hyde: A Kaplan SAT Score-Raising Classic
Wuthering Heights: A Kaplan SAT Score-Raising Classic
The War of the Worlds: A Kaplan SAT Score-Raising Classic

SAT Vocabulary Prep
Level 1

KAPLAN

PUBLISHING

New York

This publication is designed to provide accurate and authoritative information in regard to the subject matter covered. It is sold with the understanding that the publisher is not engaged in rendering legal, accounting, or other professional service. If legal advice or other expert assistance is required, the services of a competent professional should be sought.

© 2008 Kaplan, Inc.

Published by Kaplan Publishing, a division of Kaplan, Inc.
1 Liberty Plaza, 24th Floor
New York, NY 10006

Printed in the United States of America

August 2008
10 9 8 7 6 5 4

ISBN-13: 978-1-4195-5222-9

Kaplan Publishing books are available at special quantity discounts to use for sales promotions, employee premiums, or educational purposes. Please email our Special Sales Department to order or for more information at kaplanpublishing@kaplan.com, or write to Kaplan Publishing, 1 Liberty Plaza, 24th Floor, New York, NY 10006.

HOW TO USE THIS BOOK

Kaplan's *SAT Vocabulary Prep Level 1* is designed to help you learn 500 essential SAT vocabulary words in a quick and easy way.

- There are three vocabulary words on the front of each page (including parts of speech and pronunciations), and on the back you'll find the definitions, sample sentences with the SAT words in action, and synonyms of the words.

- The vocabulary words are color-coded by level of difficulty to make navigating the book easier and studying more fun.

- As a special bonus, we've included an SAT word root list at the back of this book for extra studying power.

Looking for still more SAT prep? Be sure to pick up a copy of Kaplan's *SAT Vocabulary Prep Level 2*, with 500 of the hardest words that often appear on the SAT.

Good luck!

ABDICATE
verb (<u>aab</u> duh kayt)

· ·

ABERRATION
noun (aa buhr <u>ay</u> shuhn)

· ·

ACERBIC
adj (uh <u>suhr</u> bihk)

BASIC

to give up a position, right, or power

With the angry mob clamoring outside the palace, the king **abdicated** his throne and fled.

Synonyms: cede; quit; relinquish; resign; yield

• •

something different from the usual

Due to the bizarre **aberrations** in the author's behavior, her publicist decided that the less the public saw of her, the better.

Synonyms: abnormality; anomaly; deviation; irregularity

• •

bitter, sharp in taste or temper

Gina's **acerbic** wit and sarcasm were feared around the office.

Synonyms: biting; caustic; cutting; tart

BASIC

ACQUIESCE
verb (<u>aak</u> wee ehs)

....

ADULTERATE
verb (uh <u>duhl</u> tuhr ayt)

....

AGGRANDIZE
verb (uh <u>graan</u> diez) (aa <u>gruhn</u> diez)

BASIC

to agree; to comply quietly

The princess **acquiesced** to demands that she marry a nobleman, but she was not happy about it.

Synonyms: accede; consent; submit

• •

to corrupt or make impure

The restaurateur made his ketchup last longer by **adulterating** it with water.

Synonyms: contaminate; dilute

• •

to make larger or greater in power

All the millionaire really wanted was to **aggrandize** his personal wealth as much as possible.

Synonyms: advance; elevate; exalt; glorify; magnify

ALLEGORY
noun (<u>aa</u> lih gohr ee)

· ·

ANTERIOR
adj (aan <u>teer</u> ee uhr)

· ·

ANTIPATHY
noun (aan <u>tih</u> puh thee)

BASIC

symbolic representation

The novelist used the stormy ocean as an **allegory** for her life's struggles.

Synonyms: metaphor; symbolism

· ·

preceding, previous, before, prior (to)

Following tradition, the couple's wedding was **anterior** to the honeymoon.

Synonyms: foregoing; previous

· ·

dislike, hostility; extreme opposition or aversion

The **antipathy** between the French and the English regularly erupted into open warfare.

Synonyms: antagonism; enmity; malice

ARDENT
adj (<u>ahr</u> dihnt)

....

ARDOR
noun (<u>ahr</u> duhr)

....

ASTRINGENT
adj (uh <u>strihn</u> juhnt)

passionate, enthusiastic, fervent

After a 25-game losing streak, even the Mets' most **ardent** fans realized the team wouldn't finish first.

Synonyms: fervid; intense; vehement

• •

great emotion or passion

Bishop's **ardor** for landscape was evident when he passionately described the beauty of the Hudson Valley.

Synonyms: enthusiasm; zeal

• •

harsh, severe, stern

The principal's punishments seemed overly **astringent,** but the students did not dare to complain.

Synonyms: bitter; caustic; sharp

ATROCIOUS
adj (uh <u>troh</u> shuhs)

. . . .

ATROPHY
noun (<u>aa</u> troh fee)

. . . .

AUSPICIOUS
adj (aw <u>spih</u> shuhs)

BASIC

monstrous, shockingly bad, wicked

The young boy committed the **atrocious** act of vandalizing the new community center.

Synonyms: appalling; deplorable; direful; horrible

. . . .

to waste away, wither from disuse

When Mimi stopped exercising, her muscles began to **atrophy**.

Synonyms: degenerate; deteriorate

. . . .

having favorable prospects, promising

Tamika thought that having lunch with the boss was an **auspicious** start to her new job.

Synonyms: encouraging; hopeful; positive; propitious

AVARICE
noun (<u>aa</u> vuhr ihs)

· ·

BANAL
adj (buh <u>naal</u>) (<u>bay</u> nuhl) (buh <u>nahl</u>)

· ·

BELEAGUER
verb (bih <u>lee</u> guhr)

greed

Rebecca's **avarice** motivated her to stuff the $100 bill in her pocket instead of returning it to the man who had dropped it.

Synonyms: cupidity; rapacity

••

trite, overly common

He used **banal** phrases like "Have a nice day" or "Another day, another dollar."

Synonyms: hackneyed; inane; shopworn

••

to harass, plague

Mickey **beleaguered** his parents until they finally gave in to his request for a new computer.

Synonyms: beset; besiege

BELLIGERENT
adj (buh <u>lih</u> juhr uhnt)

....

BEQUEATH
verb (bih <u>kweeth</u>) (bih <u>kweeth</u>)

....

BESEECH
verb (bih <u>seech</u>)

hostile, tending to fight

The angry customer was extremely **belligerent** despite the manager's offer to return his money.

Synonyms: agressive; bellicose; combative; pugnacious

· ·

to give or leave through a will; to hand down

Grandpa **bequeathed** the house to his daughter and the car to his son.

Synonyms: bestow; pass on; transmit

· ·

to beg, plead, implore

She **beseeched** him to give her a second chance, but he refused.

Synonyms: entreat; petition; supplicate

BILK
verb (bihlk)

....

BOON
noun

....

BREACH
noun (breech)

to cheat, defraud

Though the lawyer seemed honest, the woman feared he would try to **bilk** her out of her money.

Synonyms: dupe; fleece; swindle

• •

blessing, something to be thankful for

Dirk realized that his new coworker's computer skills would be a real **boon** to the company.

Synonyms: benefit; favor; treasure; windfall

• •

act of breaking, violation

The record company sued the singer for **breach** of contract when he recorded for another company without permission.

Synonyms: contravention; dereliction; gap; lapse; rift

BRUSQUE
adj (bruhsk)

....

CADENCE
noun (kayd ns)

....

CAJOLE
verb (kuh johl)

rough and abrupt in manner

The bank teller's **brusque** treatment of his customers soon evoked several complaints.

Synonyms: blunt; curt; gruff; rude; tactless

· ·

rhythmic flow of poetry; marching beat

Pierre spoke with a lovely **cadence**, charming all those who heard him.

Synonyms: inflection; rhythm

· ·

to flatter, coax, persuade

The spoiled girl could **cajole** her father into buying her anything.

Synonyms: blandish; wheedle

BASIC

CATHARSIS
noun (kuh <u>thahr</u> sihs)

···

CAVALIER
noun (kaav uh <u>leer</u>)

···

CENTRIPETAL
adj (sehn <u>trihp</u> ih tl)

BASIC

purification, cleansing

Plays can be more satisfying if they end in some sort of emotional **catharsis** for the characters involved.

Synonyms: purgation; release

• •

carefree, happy; with lordly disdain

The nobleman's **cavalier** attitude towards the suffering of the peasants made them hate him.

Synonym: disdainful

• •

directed or moving towards the center

It is **centripetal** force that keeps trains from derailing as they round curves.

Synonym: centralizing

CHAGRIN
noun (shuh <u>grihn</u>)

∙∙∙

CHARLATAN
noun (<u>shahr</u> luh tihn)

∙∙∙

CLANDESTINE
adj (klaan <u>dehs</u> tien)

BASIC

shame, embarrassment, humiliation

No doubt, the president felt a good deal of **chagrin** after forgetting the name of the prime minister at the state banquet.

Synonyms: discomfiture; mortification

•••

quack, fake

"That **charlatan** of a doctor prescribed the wrong medicine for me!" complained the patient.

Synonyms: fraud; humbug; imposter

•••

secretive, concealed for a darker purpose

The double agent paid many **clandestine** visits to the president's office in the dead of night.

Synonyms: covert; underground

CLEMENCY
noun (<u>kleh</u> muhn see)

· ·

COLLATERAL
adj (kuh <u>laat</u> uhr uhl)

· ·

COMELINESS
noun (<u>kuhm</u> lee nihs)

BASIC

merciful leniency

Kyle begged for **clemency**, explaining that he robbed the bank to pay for his medical bills.

Synonyms: indulgence; pardon

• •

accompanying

"Let's try to stick to the main issue here and not get into all the **collateral** questions," urged the committee leader.

Synonym: ancillary

• •

physical grace and beauty

Ann's **comeliness** made her perfect for the role of Sleeping Beauty.

Synonyms: attractiveness; seemliness

CONGENITAL
adj (kuhn <u>jehn</u> ih tl)

· ·

CONJECTURE
noun (kuhn <u>jehk</u> shuhr)

· ·

CONJURE
verb (<u>kahn</u> juhr) (kuhn j<u>oor</u>)

BASIC

existing since birth

The infant's **congenital** health problem was corrected through surgery.

Synonym: innate

• •

speculation, prediction

The actor refused to comment, forcing gossip columnists to make **conjectures** on his love life.

Synonyms: hypothesis; postulation; supposition

• •

to evoke a spirit, cast a spell

The cotton candy **conjured** up the image of the fairgrounds he used to visit as a child.

Synonym: summon

BASIC

CONSTRUE
verb (kuhn <u>stroo</u>)

· ·

CONSUMMATE
adj (<u>kahn</u> suh muht) (<u>kahn</u> soo miht)

· ·

CONVOKE
verb (kuhn <u>vohk</u>)

to explain or interpret

"I wasn't sure how to **construe** that last remark he made," said Delia, "but I suspect it was an insult."

Synonyms: analyze; translate

• •

accomplished, complete, perfect

The skater delivered a **consummate** performance, perfect in every aspect.

Synonyms: exhaustive; flawless; ideal; thorough

• •

to call together, summon

The president **convoked** a group of experts to advise him on how to deal with the crisis.

Synonyms: assemble; convene; gather

BASIC

CONVOLUTED
adj (kahn vuh <u>loo</u> tehd)

··

COPIOUS
adj (<u>koh</u> pee uhs)

··

CORROBORATE
verb (kuh <u>rahb</u> uhr ayt)

BASIC

twisted, complicated, involved

Although many people bought *A Brief History of Time*, few could follow its **convoluted** ideas and theories.

Synonyms: baroque; elaborate; intricate

· ·

abundant, plentiful

The hostess had prepared **copious** amounts of food for the banquet.

Synonyms: abounding; ample

· ·

to confirm, verify

Roberto was able to **corroborate** his friend's story by showing the receipt that proved they were indeed at a restaurant all night.

Synonyms: confirm; prove; substantiate; warrant

COUNTENANCE
noun (<u>kown</u> tuh nuhns)

· ·

CRESCENDO
noun (kruh <u>shehn</u> doh)

· ·

CULPABLE
adj (<u>kuhl</u> puh buhl)

BASIC

facial expression; look of approval or support

Jeremy was afraid of the new Music Appreciation instructor because she had such an evil **countenance**.

Synonyms: face; expression

• •

gradual increase in volume of sound

The **crescendo** of tension became unbearable as Evel Knievel prepared to jump his motorcycle over the school buses.

Synonym: progressively greater

• •

guilty, responsible for wrong

The CEO is **culpable** for the bankruptcy of the company; he was, after all, in charge of it.

Synonyms: answerable; blameworthy

CURMUDGEON
noun (kuhr <u>muh</u> juhn)

· ·

CURSORY
adj (<u>kuhr</u> suh ree)

· ·

DAUNT
verb (dawnt)

BASIC

cranky person

The old man was a notorious **curmudgeon** who snapped at anyone who disturbed him for any reason.

Synonyms: coot; crab; grouch

....

hastily done, superficial

The copyeditor gave the article a **cursory** once-over, missing dozens of errors.

Synonyms: careless; shallow

....

to discourage, intimidate

She tried hard not to let the enormity of the situation **daunt** her.

Synonyms: consternate; demoralize; dishearten

DEBASE
verb (dih <u>bays</u>)

....

DEBILITATE
verb (dih <u>bih</u> lih tayt)

....

DEBUNK
verb (dih <u>buhnk</u>)

to degrade or lower in quality or stature

The president's deceitful actions **debased** the stature of his office.

Synonyms: adulterate; defile; demean; denigrate

• •

to weaken, enfeeble

The flu d**ebilitated** the postal worker; she was barely able to finish her rounds.

Synonyms: devitalize; drain; enervate; exhaust; sap

• •

to discredit, disprove

It was the teacher's mission in life to **debunk** the myth that females are bad at math.

Synonyms: belie; confute; contradict; controvert; explode

DEFERENTIAL
adj (dehf uh <u>rehn</u> shuhl)

· ·

DEFT
adj (dehft)

· ·

DELUGE
verb (<u>dehl</u> yooj) (<u>dehl</u> yoozh) (<u>day</u> looj)
(<u>day</u> loozh) (dih <u>looj</u>) (dih <u>loozh</u>)

BASIC

respectful and polite in a submissive way

The respectful young law clerk was **deferential** to the Supreme Court justice.

Synonyms: courteous; obsequious

• •

skillful, dexterous

It was a pleasure to watch the **deft** carpenter as he repaired the furniture.

Synonyms: adept; adroit; expert; proficient; nimble

• •

to submerge, overwhelm; flood

The popular actor was **deluged** with fan mail.

Synonyms: engulf; immerse; inundate; swamp; whelm

DENIGRATE
verb (<u>deh</u> nih grayt)

....

DEPRAVITY
noun (dih <u>praav</u> ih tee)

....

DEPRECATE
verb (<u>dehp</u> rih kayt)

to slur or blacken someone's reputation

The people still loved the president, despite his enemies' attempts to **denigrate** his character.

Synonyms: belittle; disparage; malign; slander; vilify

• •

sinfulness, moral corruption

The **depravity** of the actor's Hollywood lifestyle shocked his traditional parents.

Synonyms: corruption; debauchery; decadence; degradation; enormity

• •

to belittle, disparage

Ernest **deprecated** his own contribution, instead praising the efforts of his coworkers.

Synonyms: denigrate; discount; minimize

BASIC

DEPRECIATE
verb (dih <u>pree</u> shee ayt)

· ·

DESECRATE
verb (<u>dehs</u> ih krayt)

· ·

DESPONDENT
adj (dih <u>spahn</u> duhnt)

BASIC

to lose value gradually

The Barrettas sold their house, fearful that its value would **depreciate** due to the nuclear reactor being built around the corner.

Synonym: lessen

. . . .

to abuse something sacred

The archaeologist tried to explain to the explorer that he had **desecrated** the temple by spitting in it.

Synonyms: defile; degrade; profane; violate

. . . .

discouraged, dejected

Mr. Baker was lonely and **despondent** after his wife's death.

Synonyms: dejected; depressed; desolate; forlorn; sad

DESPOT
noun (<u>dehs</u> puht) (<u>dehs</u> paht)

. . . .

DESTITUTE
adj (<u>dehs</u> tih toot) (dehs tih <u>tyoot</u>)

. . . .

DEXTEROUS
adj (<u>dehk</u> stuhr uhs) (<u>dehk</u> struhs)

BASIC

tyrannical ruler

The **despot** banished half the nobles in his court on a whim.

Synonyms: authoritarian; autocrat; dictator; totalitarian

• •

very poor, poverty-stricken

After the stock market crash, Jeanette was **destitute,** forced to beg on the streets in order to survive.

Synonyms: broke; impecunious; insolvent; needy; penurious

• •

skilled physically or mentally

The gymnast who won the contest was far more **dexterous** than the other competitors.

Synonyms: adept; adroit; deft; nimble; skilled

DIABOLICAL
adj (die uh <u>bahl</u> ih kuhl)

....

DIATRIBE
noun (<u>die</u> uh trieb)

....

DIMINUTIVE
adj (dih <u>mihn</u> yuh tihv)

fiendish, wicked

Sherlock Holmes's archenemy is the **diabolical** Professor Moriarty.

Synonym: evil

· ·

bitter verbal attack

During the CEO's lengthy **diatribe,** the board members managed to remain calm and self-controlled.

Synonyms: fulmination; harangue; jeremiad; philippic; tirade

· ·

small

Napoleon made up for his **diminutive** stature with his aggressive personality, terrifying his courtiers.

Synonyms: minscule; short; tiny; wee

DISCONCERTING
adj (dihs kuhn <u>suhr</u> tihng)

· ·

DISPARAGE
verb (dih <u>spaar</u> ihj)

· ·

DISSEMINATE
verb (dih <u>sehm</u> uh nayt)

bewildering, perplexing, slightly disturbing

Brad found his mother-in-law's hostile manner so **disconcerting** that he acted like a fool in her presence.

Synonym: upsetting

• •

to belittle, speak disrespectfully about

Gregorio loved to **disparage** his brother's dancing skills, pointing out every mistake he made on the floor.

Synonyms: denigrate; deride; derogate; ridicule

• •

to spread far and wide

The wire service **disseminates** information so rapidly that events get reported shortly after they happen.

Snonyms: circulate; diffuse; disperse

DISSENSION
noun (dih <u>sehn</u> shunhn)

. . . .

DISSIPATE
verb (<u>dihs</u> uh payt)

. . . .

DURESS
noun (duhr <u>ehs</u>)

BASIC

difference of opinion

The government was forced to abandon the extensive reforms it had planned, due to continued **dissension** within its party ranks about the form these changes should take.

Synonym: disagreement

. . . .

to scatter; to pursue pleasure to excess

The fog gradually **dissipated,** revealing all the ships docked in the harbor.

Synonyms: carouse; consume; disperse; dissolve; squander

. . . .

threat of force or intimidation; imprisonment

Under **duress,** the political dissident revealed the names of others in her organization to the secret police.

Synonyms: coercion; compulsion; constraint; pressure

EBB
verb (ehb)

....

EDICT
noun (<u>ee</u> dihkt)

....

EFFIGY
noun (<u>eh</u> fuh jee)

to fade away, recede

From her beachside cottage, Melissa enjoyed watching the tide **ebb** and flow.

Synonyms: abate; retreat; subside; wane; withdraw

• •

law, command, official public order

Pedestrians often disobey the **edict** that they should not jaywalk.

Synonyms: decree; dictuml directive; fiat; ukase

• •

stuffed doll; likeness of a person

The anti-American militants burned Uncle Sam in **effigy** during their demonstration.

Synonyms: dummy; figure; image

EGREGIOUS
adj (ih <u>gree</u> juhs)

· ·

ENTREAT
verb (ehn <u>treet</u>)

· ·

ETHEREAL
adj (ih <u>theer</u> ee uhl)

BASIC

conspicuously bad

The English textbook contained several **egregious** errors; for example, "grammar" was misspelled as "gramer" throughout.

Synonyms: blatant; flagrant; glaring; gross; rank

• •

to plead, beg

I **entreated** him to just tell me what the problem was instead of bottling it up inside, but he refused.

Synonyms: beseech; implore; importune; petition; request

• •

not earthly, spiritual, delicate

Her delicate, **ethereal** beauty made her a popular model for pre-Raphaelite artists.

Synonyms: airy; diaphanous; gossamer; intangible; sheer

EXACERBATE
verb (ihg <u>zaas</u> uhr bayt)

· ·

EXHUME
verb (ihg <u>zoom</u>) (ihg <u>zyoom</u>) (ihk <u>syoom</u>)
(ehks <u>hyoom</u>)

· ·

EXONERATE
verb (ihg <u>zahn</u> uh rayt)

BASIC

to aggravate, intensify the bad qualities of

It is unwise to take aspirin to relieve heartburn; instead of providing relief, the drug will only **exacerbate** the problem.

Synonyms: deepen; escalate; worsen

• •

to remove from a grave; uncover a secret

The archaeologist **exhumed** the scrolls from the ancient tomb.

Synonyms: disinter; unearth

• •

to clear of blame, absolve

The fugitive was **exonerated** when another criminal confessed to committing the crime.

Synonyms: acquit; exculpate; vindicate

BASIC

EXTRICATE
verb (<u>ehk</u> strih kayt)

. . . .

FASTIDIOUS
adj (faa <u>stihd</u> ee uhs) (fuh <u>stihd</u> ee uhs)

. . . .

FETID
adj (<u>feh</u> tihd)

BASIC

to free from, disentangle

The fly was unable to **extricate** itself from the flypaper.

Synonyms: disencumber; disengage; release; untangle

• •

careful with details

Brett was normally so **fastidious** that Rachel was astonished to find his desk littered with clutter.

Synonyms: meticulous; painstaking; precise; punctilious; scrupulous

• •

foul-smelling, putrid

The **fetid** stench from the outhouse caused Laura to wrinkle her nose in disgust.

Synonyms: funky; malodorous; noisome; rank; stinky

BASIC

FLACCID
adj (<u>flaa</u> sihd)

....

FORTE
noun (<u>fohr</u> tay)

....

FOUNDER
verb (<u>fown</u> duhr)

limp, flabby, weak

The woman jiggled her **flaccid** arms in disgust, resolving to begin lifting weights as soon as possible.

Synonyms: floppy; soft

· ·

strong point, something a person does well

Since math was Dan's **forte**, his friends always asked him to calculate the bill whenever they went out to dinner together.

Synonyms: métier; specialty

· ·

to fall helplessly; to sink

After colliding with the jagged rock, the ship **foundered**, forcing the crew to abandon it.

Synonyms: immerse; miscarry; plunge

FRACAS
noun (fraak uhs) (fray kuhs)

....

GARNER
verb (gahr nuhr)

....

GLOWER
verb (glow uhr)

noisy dispute

When the players discovered that the other team was cheating, a violent **fracas** ensued.

Synonyms: brawl; broil; donnybrook; fray; melee

• •

to gather and store

The director managed to **garner** financial backing from several different sources for her next project.

Synonyms: amass; acquire; glean; harvest; reap

• •

to glare, stare angrily and intensely

The cranky waitress **glowered** at the indecisive customer.

Synonyms: frown; scowl

GOAD
verb (gohd)

· ·

GRATIS
adj (grah tihs) (gray tihs)

· ·

HARBINGER
noun (haar buhn juhr)

BASIC

to prod or urge

Denise **goaded** her sister Leigh into running the marathon with her.

Synonyms: impel; incite; provoke; rouse; stimulate

• •

free, costing nothing

The college students swarmed around the **gratis** buffet in the lobby.

Synonyms: complimentary; costless

• •

precursor, sign of something to come

The groundhog's appearance on February 2 is a **harbinger** of spring.

Synonyms: forerunner; herald; omen; presage

HARROWING
adj (<u>haa</u> roh ng)

....

IMMUTABLE
adj (ihm <u>myoot</u> uh buhl)

....

IMPETUOUS
adj (ihm <u>peh</u> choo uhs)
(ihm <u>pehch</u> wuhs)

BASIC

extremely distressing, terrifying

We stayed up all night listening to Dave and Will talk about their **harrowing** adventures at sea.

Synonyms: tormenting; vexing

• •

unchangeable, invariable

Poverty was an **immutable** fact of life for the unfortunate Wood family; every moneymaking scheme they tried failed.

Synonyms: fixed; permanent; stationary; steady

• •

quick to act without thinking

The **impetuous** day trader rushed to sell his stocks at the first hint of trouble, and lost $300,000.

Synonyms: impulsive; passionate

BASIC

INDIGENT
adj (<u>ihn</u> dih juhnt)

. . . .

INDIGNANT
adj (ihn <u>dihg</u> nuhnt)

. . . .

INERT
adj (ihn <u>uhrt</u>)

BASIC

very poor

Because the suspect was **indigent,** the state paid for his legal representation.

Synonyms: destitute; impecunious; impoverished; needy; penniless

• •

angry, incensed, offended

The innocent passerby was **indignant** when the police treated him as a suspect in the crime.

Synonyms: furious; irate; ireful; mad; wrathful

• •

unable to move, tending to inactivity

In the heat of the desert afternoon, lizards lie **inert.**

Synonyms: dormant; idle; inactive; lethargic; sluggish

INGENIOUS
adj (ih <u>jeen</u> yuhs)

....

INSIDIOUS
adj (ihn <u>sihd</u> ee uhs)

....

INTERLOPER
noun (<u>ihn</u> tuhr loh puhr)

original, clever, inventive

Luther found an **ingenious** way to solve the complex math problem.

Synonyms: cunning; imaginative; shrewd

• •

sly, treacherous, devious

Iago's **insidious** comments about Desdemona fuelled Othello's feelings of jealousy regarding his wife.

Synonyms: alluring; deceitful; perfidious

• •

trespasser; meddler in others' affairs

The wolf pack rejected the lone pup as an **interloper**.

Synonym: intruder

JUGGERNAUT
noun (<u>juhg</u> uhr naht)

....

JUXTAPOSITION
noun (juk stuh puh <u>zihsh</u> uhn)

....

KNELL
noun (nehl)

huge force destroying everything in its path

The **juggernaut** of the army surged ahead until it was halted in its tracks by the brutal winter.

Synonym: overwhelming force

• •

side-by-side placement

The porcelain dog was placed in **juxtaposition** with the straw doghouse on the mantelpiece.

Synonyms: comparison; contrast

• •

sound of a funeral bell; omen of death or failure

When the townspeople heard the **knell** from the church belfry, they knew that their mayor had died.

Synonyms: chime; peal; toll

LIMPID
adj (<u>lim</u> pihd)

....

MACHINATION
noun (mahk uh <u>nay</u> shuhn)

....

MAELSTROM
noun (<u>mayl</u> struhm)

clear, transparent

Shelley could see all the way to the bottom through the pond's **limpid** water.

Synonyms: lucid; pellucid; serene

• •

plot or scheme

Tired of his employees' endless **machinations** to destroy the company, the boss had them fired.

Synonyms: cabal; conspiracy; design; intrigue

• •

whirlpool; turmoil; agitated state of mind

The transportation system of the city had collapsed in the **maelstrom** of war.

Synonyms: eddy; turbulence

MAGNANIMOUS
adj (maag <u>naan</u> uh muhs)

. . . .

MATRICULATE
verb (muh <u>trihk</u> yuh layt)

. . . .

MAUDLIN
adj (<u>mawd</u> lihn)

BASIC

generous, noble in spirit

Although at first he seemed mean, Uncle Frank turned out to be a very **magnanimous** fellow.

Synonyms: forgiving; unselfish

• •

to enroll as a member of a college or university

When Suda-May **matriculates** at Yale University this coming fall, she will move to New Haven.

Synonyms: enlist; join

• •

overly sentimental

The mother's death should have been a touching scene, but the movie's treatment of it was so **maudlin** that, instead of making the audience cry, it made them cringe.

Synonyms: mawkish; saccharine; weepy

METICULOUS
adj (mih <u>tihk</u> yuh luhs)

....

METTLE
noun (<u>meht</u> l)

....

MIRTH
noun (muhrth)

extremely careful, fastidious, painstaking

To clean every square inch of the huge mural, the restorers had to be **meticulous**.

Synonyms: finicky; fussy; precise; punctilious; scrupulous

••

courageousness; endurance

The helicopter pilot showed her **mettle** as she landed in the battlefield to rescue the wounded soldiers.

Synonyms: character; fortitude; spirit

••

frivolity, gaiety, laughter

Vera's hilarious jokes contributed to the general **mirth** at the dinner party.

Synonyms: glee; hilarity; jollity; merriment

BASIC

NEGLIGIBLE
adj (<u>nehg</u> lih jih buhl)

· ·

NOTORIETY
noun (noh tohr <u>ie eh</u> tee)

· ·

NOXIOUS
adj (nahk shuhs)

BASIC

not worth considering

It's obvious from our **negligible** dropout rate that our students love our program.

Synonyms: insignificant; nugatory; trifling; trivial

· ·

unfavorable fame

Wayne realized from the silence that greeted him as he entered the office that his **notoriety** preceded him.

Synonyms: disgrace; dishonor; disrepute; infamy; opprobrium

· ·

harmful, unwholesome

The people on the sidewalk covered their noses and mouths as the bus passed to avoid breathing in the **noxious** exhaust fumes.

Synonyms: corrupting; poisonous; toxic; unhealthy

NUANCE
noun (<u>noo</u> ahns)

· ·

NULLIFY
verb (<u>nuh</u> lih fie)

· ·

OBTUSE
adj (uhb <u>toos</u>)

shade of meaning

The scholars argued for hours over tiny **nuances** in the interpretation of the last line of the poem.

Synonyms: gradation; subtlety; tone

· ·

to make legally invalid; to counteract the effect of

Crystal **nullified** her contract with her publisher when she received a better offer from another company.

Synonyms: cancel; negate; neutralize; undo

· ·

insensitive, stupid, dull, unclear

The directions were so **obtuse** that Alfred did not understand what was expected of him.

Synonyms: blunt; dense; slow

OMNISCIENT
adj (ahm <u>nih</u> shehnt)

....

OPULENCE
noun (<u>ah</u> pyoo lehns)

....

PERDITION
noun (puhr <u>dihsh</u> uhn)

BASIC

having infinite knowledge, all-seeing

Fiction writers have the ability to be **omniscient** about the characters they create.

Synonyms: all-knowing; divine

• •

wealth

Livingston considered his expensive car to be a symbol of both **opulence** and style.

Synonyms: affluence; luxury; prosperity

• •

complete and utter loss; damnation

Faust brought **perdition** upon himself when he made a deal with the Devil in exchange for power.

Synonym: abyss

PERFUNCTORY
adj (puhr fuhnk tor ee)

··

PERMEABLE
adj (puhr mee uh buhl)

··

PESTILENCE
noun (peh stihl ehns)

BASIC

done in a routine way; indifferent

The machinelike bank teller processed the transaction and gave the waiting customer a **perfunctory** smile.

Synonyms: careless; halfhearted; tepid

· ·

penetrable

Karen discovered that her raincoat was **permeable** when she was drenched while wearing it in a rainstorm.

Synonyms: pervious; porous

· ·

epidemic, plague

The country went into national crisis when it was plagued by both **pestilence** and floods at the same time.

Synonyms: contagion; disease; illness; scourge; sickness

PETULANCE
noun (<u>peh</u> chu luhns)

· ·

PILFER
verb (<u>pihl</u> fuhr)

· ·

PITHY
adj (<u>pih</u> thee)

BASIC

rudeness, peevishness

The child's **petulance** annoyed the teacher, who liked her students to be cheerful and cooperative.

Synonyms: fretfulness; irritability; querulousness; testiness

• •

to steal

Marianne did not **pilfer** the money for herself but rather for her sick brother, who needed medicine.

Synonyms: arrogate; embezzle; filch; poach; purloin

• •

profound, substantial; concise, succinct, to the point

Martha's **pithy** comments during the interview must have been impressive, because she got the job.

Synonyms: brief; compact; laconic; terse

PITTANCE
noun (<u>piht</u> ns)

....

PLACATE
verb (<u>play</u> cayt)

....

PREDILECTION
noun (preh dih <u>lehk</u> shuhn)

meager amount or wage

Zack felt sure he would not be able to buy food for his family with the small **pittance** the government gave him.

Synonyms: insufficiency; scrap

• •

to soothe or pacify

The burglar tried to **placate** the snarling Doberman by saying, "Nice doggy," and offering it a treat.

Synonyms: appease; conciliate; mollify

• •

preference, liking

The old woman's **predilection** for candy was evident from the chocolate bar wrappers strewn all over her apartment.

Synonyms: bias; leaning; partiality; penchant; proclivity

PROCLIVITY
noun (proh <u>clih</u> vuh tee)

· ·

PUERILE
adj (<u>pyoo</u> ruhl)

· ·

PUGILISM
noun (<u>pyoo</u> juhl ih suhm)

tendency, inclination

His **proclivity** for speeding got him into trouble with the highway patrol on many occasions.

Synonyms: partiality; penchant; predilection; predisposition; propensity

• •

childish, immature, silly

His **puerile** antics are really annoying; sometimes he acts like a five-year-old!

Synonyms: infantile; jejune; juvenile

• •

boxing

Pugilism has been defended as a positive outlet for aggressive impulses.

Synonyms: fighting; sparring

PUGNACIOUS
adj (pug <u>nay</u> shus)

....

RECANT
verb (ree <u>kant</u>)

....

REMEDIABLE
adj (rih <u>mee</u> dee uh buhl)

BASIC

quarrelsome, eager and ready to fight

The serene eighty-year-old used to be a **pugnacious** troublemaker in her youth, but she's softer now.

Synonyms: bellicose; belligerent; contentious

• •

to retract a statement, opinion, etc.

The statement was so damaging that the politician had no hopes of recovering his credibility, even though he tried to **recant** the words.

Synonyms: disavow; disclaim; disown; renounce; repudiate

• •

capable of being corrected

In the belief that the juvenile delinquent was **remediable** and not a hardened criminal, the judge put him on probation.

Synonym: fixable

BASIC

RETICENT
adj (<u>reh</u> tih suhnt)

....

RETIRING
adj (rih <u>tier</u> ihng)

....

REVELRY
noun (<u>reh</u> vuhl ree)

not speaking freely; reserved

Physically small and **reticent,** Joan Didion often went unnoticed by those upon whom she was reporting.

Synonyms: restrained; secretive; silent; taciturn

• •

shy, modest, reserved

A shy and **retiring** man, Chuck was horrified at the idea of having to speak in public.

Synonym: timid

• •

boisterous festivity

An atmosphere of **revelry** filled the school after its basketball team's surprising victory.

Synonyms: cavorting; frolic; gaiety; jollity; merrymaking

RIBALD
adj (<u>rih</u> buhld)

· ·

RUMINATE
verb (<u>roo</u> muh nayt)

· ·

SENTIENT
adj (<u>sehn</u> shuhnt)

BASIC

humorous in a vulgar way

The court jester's **ribald** brand of humor delighted the rather uncouth king.

Synonyms: coarse; gross; indelicate; lewd; obscene

• •

to contemplate, reflect upon

The scholars spent days at the retreat **ruminating** upon the complexities of the geopolitical situation.

Synonyms: deliberate; meditate; mull; muse; ponder

• •

aware, conscious, able to perceive

Despite his complete lack of sleep, Jorge was still **sentient** when I spoke to him this morning.

Synonyms: feeling; intelligent; thinking

BASIC

SERAPHIC
adj (seh rah fihk)

....

SIMPER
verb (sihm puhr)

....

SINUOUS
adj (sihn yoo uhs)

angelic, pure, sublime

Selena's sweet, **seraphic** appearance belied her nasty, bitter personality.

Synonyms: cherubic; heavenly

• •

to smirk, smile foolishly

The spoiled girl **simpered** as her mother praised her extravagantly to the guests at the party.

Synonyms: grin; smirk

• •

winding; intricate, complex

Thick, **sinuous** vines wound around the trunk of the tree.

Synonyms: curvilinear; devious; lithe; serpentine; supple

STAID
adj (stayd)

....

STOIC
adj (<u>stoh</u> ihk)

....

SUBTERFUGE
noun (<u>suhb</u> tuhr fyooj)

self-restrained to the point of dullness

The lively young girl felt bored in the company of her **staid**, conservative date.

Synonyms: grave; sedate; serious; sober; solemn

• •

indifferent to or unaffected by emotions

While most of the mourners wept, the dead woman's husband kept up a **stoic**, unemotional facade.

Synonyms: impassive; stolid

• •

trick or tactic used to avoid something

Spies who are not skilled in the art of **subterfuge** are generally exposed before too long.

Synonyms: ruse; stratagem

SURREPTITIOUS
adj (<u>suh</u> rehp <u>tih</u> shuhs)

· ·

SYCOPHANT
noun (<u>sie</u> kuh fuhnt)

· ·

TACIT
adj (<u>taa</u> siht)

BASIC

characterized by secrecy

The queen knew nothing of the **surreptitious** plots being hatched against her at court.

Synonyms: clandestine; covert; furtive

• •

self-serving flatterer, yes-man

Dreading criticism, the actor surrounded himself with admirers and **sycophants**.

Synonyms: bootlicker; fawner; lickspittle; toady

• •

silently understood or implied

Although not a word had been said, everyone in the room knew that a **tacit** agreement had been made about which course of action to take.

Synonyms: implicit; unspoken

TANGENTIAL
adj (taan <u>jehn</u> shuhl)

....

TOME
noun (tohm)

....

TREPIDATION
noun (treh pih <u>day</u> shuhn)

BASIC

digressing, diverting

Your argument is interesting, but it's **tangential** to the matter at hand, so I suggest we get back to the point.

Synonyms: digressive; extraneous; inconsequential; irrelevant; peripheral

. . . .

book, usually large and academic

The teacher was forced to refer to various **tomes** to find the answer to the advanced student's question.

Synonyms: codex; volume

. . . .

fear and anxiety

Alana approached the door of the principal's office with **trepidation**.

Synonyms: alarm; apprehension; dread; fright

TRIFLING
adj (<u>trie</u> fling)

....

TRITE
adj (triet)

....

TRUNCATE
verb (<u>truhnk</u> ayt)

of slight worth, trivial, insignificant

That little glitch in the computer program is a **trifling** error; in general, it works very well.

Synonyms: frivolous; idle; paltry; petty; picayune

• •

shallow, superficial

Lindsay's graduation speech was the same **trite** nonsense we have heard hundreds of times in the past.

Synonyms: banal; hackneyed; shopworn; stale; threadbare

• •

to cut off, shorten by cutting

The mayor **truncated** his standard lengthy speech when he realized that the audience was not in the mood to listen to it.

Synonyms: crop; curtail; lop

USURP
verb (yoo <u>suhrp</u>)

....

UTILITARIAN
adj (yoo tih lih <u>teh</u> ree uhn)

....

VACILLATE
verb (<u>vaa</u> sihl ayt)

BASIC

to seize by force

The vice-principal was power-hungry, and threatened to **usurp** the principal's power.

Synonyms: appropriate; arrogate; assume; preempt

• •

efficient, functional, useful

The suitcase was undeniably **utilitarian,** with its convenient compartments of different sizes.

Synonyms: practical; pragmatic

• •

to waver, show indecision

The customer held up the line as he **vacillated** between ordering chocolate or coffee ice cream.

Synonyms: falter; hesitate; oscillate; sway; waffle

BASIC

VACUOUS
adj (<u>vaa</u> kyoo uhs)

······································

VAPID
adj (<u>vaa</u> pihd)

······································

VESTIGE
noun (<u>veh</u> stihj)

empty, void; lacking intelligence, purposeless

The congresswoman's **vacuous** speech angered the voters, who were tired of hearing empty platitudes.

Synonyms: idle; inane; stupid; vacant

• •

tasteless, dull

Todd found his blind date **vapid** and boring, and couldn't wait to get away from her.

Synonyms: inane; insipid; vacuous

• •

trace, remnant

Vestiges of the former tenant still remained in the apartment, although he hadn't lived there for years.

Synonyms: relic; remains; sign

VIRTUOSO
noun (vihr choo <u>oh</u> soh)

· ·

VITRIOLIC
adj (vih tree <u>ah</u> lihk)

· ·

WHET
verb (weht)

someone with masterly skill; expert musician

He is a **virtuoso** conductor and has performed in all the most prestigious concert halls.

Synonyms: genius; master

• •

burning, caustic; sharp, bitter

Given the opportunity to critique his enemy's new book, the spiteful critic wrote an unusually **vitriolic** review of it for the newspaper.

Synonyms: acerbic; scathing

• •

to sharpen, stimulate

The delicious odors wafting from the kitchen **whet** Jack's appetite, and he couldn't wait to eat.

Synonyms: hone; grind; strop

BASIC

WHIMSICAL
adj (<u>wihm</u> sih cuhl)

....

WIZENED
adj (<u>wih</u> zuhnd)

....

XENOPHOBIA
noun (zee noh <u>foh</u> bee uh)

BASIC

playful or fanciful idea

The ballet was **whimsical**, delighting the children with its imaginative characters and unpredictable sets.

Synonyms: capricious; chameleonic; erratic; fickle; mutable

• •

withered, shriveled, wrinkled

The **wizened** old man was told that the plastic surgery necessary to make him look young again would cost more money than he could imagine.

Synonyms: atrophied; desiccated; gnarled; mummified; wasted

• •

fear or hatred of foreigners or strangers

Countries in which **xenophobia** is prevalent often have more restrictive immigration policies than countries which are more accepting of foreign influences.

Synonyms: bigotry; chauvinism; prejudice

BASIC

ZEALOT
noun (<u>zeh</u> luht)

· ·

someone passionately devoted to a cause

The **zealot** had no time for those who failed to share his strongly held beliefs.

Synonyms: enthusiast; fanatic; militant; radical

· ·

ABASE
verb (uh <u>bays</u>)

....

ABJECT
adj (<u>aab</u> jehkt)

....

ABSTRUSE
adj (<u>aab</u> stroos) (<u>uhb</u> stroos)

INTERMEDIATE

to humble; to disgrace

After his immature behavior, John **abased** himself in my eyes.

Synonyms: demean; humiliate

• •

miserable, pitiful

When we found the **abject** creature lying on the ground, we took it inside and tended to its broken leg.

Synonyms: lamentable; pathetic; sorry

• •

difficult to comprehend

The philosopher's elucidation was so clear that he turned an **abstruse** subject into one his audience could grasp.

Synonyms: complex; esosteric; profound

INTERMEDIATE

AESTHETIC
adj (ehs theh tihk)

....

ALACRITY
noun (uh laak crih tee)

....

AMALGAMATE
verb (uh maal guh mayt)

INTERMEDIATE

pertaining to beauty or art

The museum curator, with her fine **aesthetic** sense, created an exhibit that was a joy to behold.

Synonyms: artistic; tasteful

• •

cheerful willingness, eagerness; speed

The eager dog fetched with **alacrity** the stick that had been tossed for him.

Synonyms: briskness; celerity; dispatch

• •

to mix, combine

Giant Industries **amalgamated** with Mega Products to form Giant-Mega Products Incorporated.

Synonyms: assimilate; incorporate; integrate; league; merge

INTERMEDIATE

AMORTIZE
verb (<u>aam</u> uhr tiiz) (uh <u>mohr</u> tiez)

....

ANACHRONISM
noun (uh <u>naak</u> ruh nih suhm)

....

ANCILLARY
adj (<u>aan</u> suhl eh ree)

to diminish by installment payments

She was able to **amortize** her debts by paying a small amount each month.

Synonym: extinguish

• •

something chronologically inappropriate

The aged hippie used **anachronisms** like "groovy" and "far out" that had not been popular for years.

Synonyms: anomalous; inappropriate; inconsistent

• •

accessory; subordinate; helping

Reforms were instituted at the main factory, but not at its **ancillary** plants, so defects continued to occur.

Synonyms: addtional; adjunct; auxiliary; supplemental

INTERMEDIATE

ARDUOUS
adj (<u>ahr</u> jyoo uhs) (<u>aar</u> dyoo uhs)

. . . .

ASSIDUOUS
adj (uh <u>sih</u> dee uhs)

. . . .

ASSUAGE
verb (uh <u>swayj</u>) (uh <u>swayzh</u>)
(uh <u>swahzh</u>)

extremely difficult, laborious

Amy thought she would pass out after completing the **arduous** climb up the mountain.

Synonyms: burdensome; hard; onerous; toilsome

•••

diligent, persistent, hard-working

The **assiduous** chauffeur scrubbed the limousine endlessly, hoping to make a good impression on his employer.

Synonyms: industrious; steadfast; thorough

•••

to make less severe, ease, relieve

Like many people, Philip Larkin used warm milk to **assuage** his sleeplessness.

Synonyms: alleviate; appease; ease; mitigate; mollify

INTERMEDIATE

AUGUST
adj (aw <u>guhst</u>)

....

BALEFUL
adj (<u>bayl</u> fuhl)

....

BASTION
noun (<u>baas</u> chyuhn) (<u>baas</u> tee uhn)

INTERMEDIATE

dignified, awe inspiring, venerable

The **august** view of the summit of the Grand Teton filled the climbers with awe.

Synonyms: admirable; awesome; grand; majestic

· ·

harmful, with evil intentions

The sullen teenager gave his nagging mother a **baleful** look.

Synonyms: dark; sinister

· ·

fortification, stronghold

The club was well known as a **bastion** of conservative values in the liberal city.

Synonyms: bulwark; defense; haven

BELABOR
verb (bih <u>lay</u> buhr)

....

BELIE
verb (bih <u>lie</u>)

....

BLANDISH
verb (<u>blaan</u> dihsh)

to insist repeatedly or harp on

I understand completely; you do not need to **belabor** the point.

Synonyms: dwell upon; lambaste

· ·

to misrepresent; expose as false

The first lady's carefree appearance **belied** rumors that she was on the verge of divorcing her husband.

Synonyms: distort; refute

· ·

to coax with flattery

We **blandished** the teacher with compliments until he finally agreed to postpone the exam.

Synonyms: cajole; charm; wheedle

BLIGHT
verb (bliet)

. . . .

BOURGEOIS
adj (boor <u>zhwaa</u>) (<u>boo</u> zhwaa)
(<u>buh</u> zhwaa)

. . . .

BURGEON
verb (<u>buhr</u> juhn)

to afflict, destroy

The farmers feared that the previous night's frost had **blighted** the potato crops entirely.

Synonyms: damage; plague

· ·

middle class

The **bourgeois** family was horrified when the lower-class family moved in next door.

Synonyms: capitalist; conventional

· ·

to sprout or flourish

Because the population of the city is **burgeoning**, we are going to need a major subway expansion.

Synonyms: blossom; expand; grow; proliferatel; thrive

INTERMEDIATE

BUTTRESS
verb (<u>buh</u> trihs)

....

CALLOW
adj (<u>kaa</u> loh)

....

CAPRICIOUS
adj (kuh <u>pree</u> shuhs) (kuh <u>prih</u> shuhs)

INTERMEDIATE

to reinforce or support

The construction workers attempted to **buttress** the ceiling with pillars.

Synonyms: bolster; brace; prop; strengthen

• •

immature, lacking sophistication

The young and **callow** fans hung on every word the talk show host said.

Synonyms: artless; ingenuous; naïve

• •

impulsive, whimsical, without much thought

Queen Elizabeth I was quite **capricious**; her courtiers could never be sure who would catch her fancy.

Synonyms: erratic; fickle; flighty; inconstant; wayward

INTERMEDIATE

CATHOLIC
adj (<u>kaa</u> thuh lihk) (<u>kaa</u> thlihk)

···

CHOLERIC
adj (<u>kah</u> luhr ihk)

···

CIRCUMSCRIBE
verb (<u>suhr</u> kuhm skrieb)

universal; broad and comprehensive

Hot tea with honey is a **catholic** remedy for a sore throat.

Synonyms: extensive; general

. . . .

easily angered, short-tempered

The **choleric** principal raged at the students who had come late to school.

Synonyms: irate; irritable; surly; wrathful

. . . .

to encircle; set limits on, confine

Diego Buenaventura's country estate is **circumscribed** by rolling hills.

Synonyms: limit; surround

INTERMEDIATE

CIRCUMSPECT
adj (suhr kuhm <u>spehkt</u>)

....

COLLOQUY
noun (<u>kahl</u> uh kwee)

....

COMMENSURATE
adj (kuh <u>mehn</u> suhr ayt)

cautious, wary

His failures have made Jack far more **circumspect** in his exploits than he used to be.

Synonyms: careful; chary; prudent

· ·

dialogue or conversation, conference

The congressmen held a **colloquy** to determine how to proceed with the environmental legislation.

Synonym: discussion

· ·

proportional

Steve was given a salary **commensurate** with his experience.

Synonyms: comparable; corresponding

INTERMEDIATE

COMPUNCTION
noun (kuhm <u>puhnk</u> shuhn)

· ·

CONGRUITY
noun (kuhn <u>groo</u> ih tee)

· ·

CONSONANT
adj (<u>kahn</u> suh nuhnt)

feeling of uneasiness caused by guilt or regret

Her **compunction** was intense when she realized that she forgot to send her best friend a birthday card.

Synonyms: dubiety; qualm; scruple

· ·

correspondence, harmony, agreement

There was an obvious **congruity** between Marco's pleasant personality and his kind actions towards others.

Synonym: accord

· ·

consistent with, in agreement with

The pitiful raise Ingrid received was **consonant** with the low opinion her manager had of her performance.

Synonyms: accordant; compatible; congruous

INTERMEDIATE

CONTINENCE
noun (<u>kahn</u> tih nihns)

....

CONVIVIAL
adj (kuhn <u>vihv</u> ee uhl)

....

CORPULENCE
noun (<u>kohr</u> pyuh luhns)

self-control, self-restraint

Lucy exhibited impressive **continence** in steering clear of fattening foods, and she lost 50 pounds.

Synonyms: discipline; moderation

• •

sociable; fond of eating, drinking, and people

The restaurant's **convivial** atmosphere contrasted starkly with the gloom of Maureen's empty apartment.

Synonym: companionable

• •

obesity, fatness, bulkiness

Egbert's **corpulence** increased as he spent several hours each day eating and drinking.

Synonyms: plumpness; portliness; rotundity; stoutness

INTERMEDIATE

CRAVEN
adj (<u>kray</u> vuhn)

. . . .

CREDENCE
noun (<u>kreed</u> ns)

. . . .

CREDULOUS
adj (<u>kreh</u> juh luhs)

cowardly

The **craven** lion cringed in the corner of his cage, terrified of the mouse.

Synonyms: faint-hearted; spineless; timid

• •

acceptance of something as true or real

Mr. Bagley couldn't give any **credence** to the charge that his darling son had cheated on his test.

Synonym: credibility

• •

gullible, trusting

Although some 4-year-olds believe in the Easter Bunny, only the most **credulous** 9-year-olds do.

Synonyms: naïve; uncritical

DECIDUOUS
adj (dih <u>sih</u> joo uhs)

....

DECOROUS
adj (<u>deh</u> kuhr uhs) (deh <u>kohr</u> uhs)

....

DECRY
verb (dih <u>crie</u>)

INTERMEDIATE

losing leaves in the fall; short-lived, temporary

Deciduous trees are bare in winter, which is why coniferous trees such as evergreens are used during winter holidays.

Synonym: ephemeral

• •

proper, tasteful, socially correct

The socialite trained her daughters in the finer points of **decorous** behavior, hoping they would make a good impression at the debutante ball.

Synonyms: appropriate; comme il faut; courteous; polite

• •

to belittle; to openly condemn

Governments all over the world **decried** the dictators' vicious massacre of the helpless citizens.

Synonyms: depreciate; deride; derogate; disparage; minimize

INTERMEDIATE

DELETERIOUS
adj (dehl ih <u>teer</u> ee uhs)

....

DELINEATION
noun (dih lihn ee <u>ay</u> shuhn)

....

DEPOSE
verb (dih <u>pohs</u>)

harmful, destructive, detrimental

If we put these defective clocks on the market, it could be quite **deleterious** to our reputation.

Synonyms: adverse; hurtful; inimical; injurious

• •

depiction, representation

Mrs. Baxter was very satisfied with the artist's **delineation** of her new mansion.

Synonyms: figuration; illustration; picture; portraiture

• •

to remove from a high position

After he was **deposed** from his throne, the king spent the rest of his life in exile.

Synonyms: dethrone; displace; overthrow; topple; unseat

DIAPHANOUS
adj (die <u>aaf</u> uh nuhs)

. . . .

DICHOTOMY
noun (die <u>kah</u> tuh mee)

. . . .

DIDACTIC
adj (die <u>daak</u> tihk)

INTERMEDIATE

allowing light to show through; delicate

Ginny's **diaphanous** gown failed to disguise the fact that she was wearing ripped panty hose.

Synonyms: gauzy; tenuous; translucent; transparent; sheer

• •

division into two parts

Westerns often feature a simple **dichotomy** between good guys and bad guys.

Synonyms: bifurcation; distinction; opposition; split

• •

excessively instructive

The father was overly **didactic** with his children, turning every activity into a lesson.

Synonyms: educational; improving; moralistic

INTERMEDIATE

DISCORDANT
adj (dihs <u>kohr</u> duhnt)

· ·

DISTEND
verb (dih <u>stehnd</u>)

· ·

DIVINE
verb (dih <u>vien</u>)

INTERMEDIATE

disagreeing; at variance

The feelings about the child's education were becoming more and more **discordant**.

Synonyms: cacophonous; dissonant; inharmonious

• •

to swell, inflate, bloat

Her stomach **distended** after she gorged on the six-course meal.

Synonyms: broaden, bulge

• •

to foretell or know by inspiration

The fortune-teller **divined** from the pattern of the tea leaves that her customer would marry five times.

Synonyms: auger; foresee; intuit; predict; presage

DIVISIVE
adj (dih <u>vie</u> sihv) (dih <u>vih</u> sihv)
(dih <u>vih</u> zihv)

· ·

DOLEFUL
adj (<u>dohl</u> fuhl)

· ·

DROLL
adj (drohl)

creating disunity or conflict

The leader used **divisive** tactics to pit his enemies against each other.

Synonyms: controversial; disruptive; sensitive

. . . .

sad, mournful

Looking into the **doleful** eyes of the lonely pony, the girl decided to take him home with her.

Synonyms: dejected; woeful

. . . .

amusing in a wry, subtle way

Although the play couldn't be described as hilarious, it was certainly **droll**.

Synonyms: comic; entertaining; funny; risible; witty

INTERMEDIATE

DULCET
adj (<u>duhl</u> suht)

· ·

EBULLIENT
adj (<u>ih</u> byool yuhnt) (<u>ih</u> buhl yuhnt)

· ·

EDIFY
verb (<u>eh</u> duh fie)

pleasant sounding, soothing to the ear

The **dulcet** tone of her voice lulled me to sleep.

Synonyms: agreeable; harmonious; melodious; sweet

· ·

exhilarated, full of enthusiasm and high spirits

The **ebullient** child exhausted the baby-sitter, who lacked the energy to keep up with her.

Synonyms: ardent; avid; bubbly; zestful

· ·

to instruct morally and spiritually

The guru was paid to **edify** the actress in the ways of Buddhism.

Synonyms: enlighten; educate; guide; teach

EFFUSIVE
adj (ih <u>fyoo</u> sihv) (eh <u>fyoo</u> sihv)
(eh <u>fyoo</u> zihv)

· ·

EGRESS
noun (<u>ee</u> grehs)

· ·

ENGENDER
verb (ehn <u>gehn</u> duhr)

INTERMEDIATE

expressing emotion without restraint

The teacher's praise for Brian's brilliant essays was **effusive**.

Synonyms: gushy; overflowing; profuse

· ·

exit

Commuter trains should have points of convenient **egress** so that during rush hour, passengers can leave the train easily.

Synonym: outlet

· ·

to produce, cause, bring about

Witnessing the patriotic speech **engendered** Tom's national pride.

Synonyms: generate; originate; procreate; propagate

INTERMEDIATE

ENMITY
noun (<u>ehn</u> muh tee)

· ·

ENSCONCE
verb (ehn <u>skahns</u>)

· ·

EPHEMERAL
adj (ih <u>fehm</u> uhr uhl)

hostility, antagonism, ill will

Despite the fact that no one remembered the offense, the **enmity** between the families continued for hundreds of years.

Synonyms: animosity; animus; antipathy; rancor

• •

to settle comfortably into a place

Wayne sold the big, old family house and **ensconced** his aged mother in a cozy little cottage.

Synonym: settle

• •

momentary, transient, fleeting

The lives of mayflies seem **ephemeral** to us, since the flies' average life span is a matter of hours.

Synonyms: evanescent; fugitive; momentary; transitory

ESOTERIC
adj (eh suh <u>tehr</u> ihk)

· ·

EXCULPATE
verb (<u>ehk</u> skuhl payt) (ihk <u>skuhl</u> payt)

· ·

EXHORT
verb (ihg <u>zohrt</u>)

understood by only a learned few

Only a handful of experts are knowledgeable about the **esoteric** world of particle physics.

Synonyms: arcane; mysterious; occult; recondite; secret

• •

to clear of blame or fault, vindicate

The legal system is intended to convict those who are guilty and to **exculpate** those who are innocent.

Synonyms: acquit; exonerate

• •

to urge or incite by strong appeals

Rob's friends **exhorted** him to beware of ice on the roads when he insisted on driving home in the middle of a snowstorm.

Synonyms: convince; inspire; press; prod; provoke

EXIGENT
adj (<u>ehk</u> suh juhnt)

· ·

EXPEDIENT
adj (ihk <u>spee</u> dee uhnt)

· ·

EXTEMPORANEOUS
adj (ihk stehm puh <u>ray</u> nee uhs)

urgent; excessively demanding

The tank was losing gasoline so rapidly that it was **exigent** to stop the source of the leak.

Synonyms: compelling; critical; crucial; imperative; pressing

• •

convenient, efficient, practical

It was more **expedient** to send the fruit directly to the retailer instead of through a middleman.

Synonyms: appropriate; sensible; useful

• •

unrehearsed, on the spur of the moment

Jan gave an **extemporaneous** performance of a Monty Python skit at her surprise birthday party.

Synonyms: ad-lib; impromptu; spontaneous; unprepared

FALLOW
adj (<u>faa</u> loh)

....

FATUOUS
adj (<u>faach</u> oo uhs)

....

FECUND
adj (<u>fee</u> kuhn) (<u>fehk</u> uhnd)

uncultivated, unused

This field should lie **fallow** for a year so that the soil does not become completely depleted.

Synonyms: idle; inactive; unseeded

· ·

stupid; foolishly self-satisfied

Ted's **fatuous** comments always embarrassed his keen-witted wife.

Synonyms: absurd; ludicrous; preposterous; ridiculous; silly

· ·

fertile, fruitful, productive

The **fecund** woman gave birth to a total of twenty children.

Synonyms: flourishing; prolific

INTERMEDIATE

FELICITOUS
adj (fih <u>lihs</u> ih tuhs)

....

FERVID
adj (<u>fuhr</u> vihd)

....

FETTER
verb (<u>feh</u> tuhr)

suitable, appropriate; well spoken

The father of bride made a **felicitous** speech at the wedding, contributing to the success of the event.

Synonym: fitting

. . . .

passionate, intense, zealous

The fans of Maria Callas were particularly **fervid**, doing anything to catch a glimpse of the great singer.

Synonyms: ardent; avid; eager; enthusiastic; vehement

. . . .

to bind, chain, confine

Lorna **fettered** the bikes together so that it was less likely that they would be stolen.

Synonyms: curb; handcuff; manacle; shackle; tether

INTERMEDIATE

FOIBLE
noun (<u>foy</u> buhl)

. . . .

FORBEARANCE
noun (fohr <u>baar</u> uhns)

. . . .

FORSWEAR
verb (fohr <u>swayr</u>)

INTERMEDIATE

INTERMEDIATE

minor weakness or character flaw

Her habit of always arriving late is just a **foible**, although it is somewhat rude.

Synonyms: blemish; failing; fault; frailty; vice

· ·

patience, restraint, leniency

Collette decided to exercise **forbearance** with her assistant's numerous errors in light of the fact that he was new on the job.

Synonyms: long-suffering; resignation; tolerance

· ·

to repudiate, renounce, disclaim, reject

I was forced to **forswear** French fries after the doctor told me that my cholesterol was too high.

Synonym: abjure

FRACTIOUS
adj (<u>fraak</u> shuhs)

. . . .

GARRULOUS
adj (<u>gaar</u> uh luhs) (<u>gaar</u> yuh luhs)

. . . .

GLIB
adj (glihb)

unruly, rebellious

The general had a hard time maintaining discipline among his **fractious** troops.

Synonyms: contentious; cranky; peevish; quarrelsome

• •

very talkative

The **garrulous** parakeet distracted its owner with its continuous talking.

Synonyms: chatty; loquacious; prolix; verbose; voluble

• •

fluent in an insincere manner; offhand, casual

The slimy politician managed to continue gaining supporters because he was a **glib** speaker.

Synonyms: easy; superficial

INTERMEDIATE

GUILE
noun (<u>gie</u> uhl)

· ·

HAPLESS
adj (<u>haap</u> luhs)

· ·

HERMETIC
adj (huhr <u>meh</u> tihk)

trickery, deception

Greg used considerable **guile** to acquire his rent-controlled apartment, even claiming to be a Vietnam Vet.

Synonyms: artifice; cunning; duplicity; wiliness

• •

unfortunate, having bad luck

I wish someone would give that poor, **hapless** soul some food and shelter.

Synonyms: ill-fated; ill-starred; luckless; jinxed; unlucky

• •

tightly sealed

The **hermetic** seal of the jar proved impossible to break.

Synonyms: airtight; impervious; watertight

INTERMEDIATE

HINTERLAND
noun (<u>hihn</u> tuhr laand)

· ·

HYPERBOLE
noun (hie <u>puhr</u> boh lee)

· ·

ICONOCLAST
noun (ie <u>kahn</u> uh klaast)

INTERMEDIATE

wilderness

The anthropologists noticed that the people had moved out of the cities and into the **hinterland**.

Synonyms: backcountry; frontier

• •

purposeful exaggeration for effect

When the mayor claimed his town was one of the seven wonders of the world, outsiders classified his statement as **hyperbole**.

Synonyms: embellishment; inflation; magnification

• •

one who attacks traditional beliefs

His lack of regard for traditional beliefs soon established him as an **iconoclast**.

Synonyms: dissident; nonconformist; rebel

IDIOSYNCRASY
noun (ih dee uh <u>sihn</u> kruh see)

· ·

ILK
noun (ihlk)

· ·

IMBUE
verb (ihm <u>byoo</u>)

INTERMEDIATE

peculiarity of temperament, eccentricity

His numerous **idiosyncrasies** included a fondness for wearing bright green shoes with mauve socks.

Synonyms: humor; oddity; quirk

• •

type or kind

"I try not to associate with men of his **ilk**," sniffed the respectable old lady.

Synonyms: character; class; nature; sort; variety

• •

to infuse; to dye, wet, moisten

Marcia struggled to **imbue** her children with decent values, a difficult task in this day and age.

Synonyms: charge; freight; impregnate; permeate; pervade

IMPERVIOUS
adj (ihm <u>puhr</u> vee uhs)

....

IMPUGN
verb (ihm <u>pyoon</u>)

....

INCENDIARY
adj (ihn <u>sehn</u> dee ehr ee)

INTERMEDIATE

impossible to penetrate; incapable of being affected

A good raincoat should be **impervious** to moisture.

Synonyms: callous; immune

• •

to call into question, attack verbally

"How dare you **impugn** my honorable motives?" protested the lawyer on being accused of ambulance chasing.

Synonyms: challenge; dispute

• •

combustible, flammable, burning easily

Gasoline is so **incendiary** that cigarette smoking is forbidden at gas stations.

Synonyms: explosive; inflammable

INTERMEDIATE

INCURSION
noun (ihn <u>kuhr</u> zhuhn) (ihn <u>kuhr</u> shuhn)

....

INDEFATIGABLE
adj (ihn dih <u>faat</u> ih guh buhl)

....

INDOLENT
adj (<u>ihn</u> duh luhnt)

INTERMEDIATE

sudden invasion

The army was unable to resist the **incursion** of the rebel forces into their territory.

Synonym: raid

. . . .

never tired

Theresa seemed **indefatigable,** barely sweating after a 10-mile run.

Synonyms: inexhaustible; unflagging; weariless

. . . .

habitually lazy, idle

Her **indolen**t ways got her fired from many jobs.

Synonyms: fainéant; languid; lethargic; slothful; sluggish

INIQUITY
noun (ih <u>nihk</u> wih tee)

· ·

INTERDICT
verb (ihn tuhr <u>dihkt</u>)

· ·

INTERPOSE
verb (ihn tuhr <u>pohz</u>)

INTERMEDIATE

sin, evil act

The principal believed that the **iniquity** the student committed was grounds for expulsion.

Synonyms: enormity; immorality; injustice; vice; wickedness

• •

to forbid, prohibit

The matron **interdicted** male visits to the girls' dorm rooms after midnight.

Synonyms: ban; outlaw

• •

to insert; to intervene

The policeman **interposed** himself between the two men who were about to start fighting.

Synonym: interfere

LACONIC
adj (luh <u>kah</u> nihk)

....

LAGGARD
noun (<u>laag</u> uhrd)

....

LASSITUDE
noun (<u>laas</u> ih tood)

INTERMEDIATE

using few words

She was a **laconic** poet who built her reputation on using words as sparingly as possible.

Synonyms: concise; pithy; succinct; terse

•••

dawdler, loafer, lazy person

The manager hesitated to fire Biff, his incompetent **laggard** of an assistant, because Biff was the CEO's son.

Synonym: slowpoke

•••

lethargy, sluggishness

The defeated French army plunged into a state of depressed **lassitude** as they trudged home from Russia.

Synonyms: listlessness; stupor; torpor; weariness

LIONIZE
verb (<u>lie</u> uhn iez)

. . . .

LISSOME
adj (<u>lihs</u> uhm)

. . . .

MERCURIAL
adj (muhr <u>kyoor</u> ee uhl)

INTERMEDIATE

to treat as a celebrity

After the success of his novel, the author was **lionized** by the press.

Synonyms: feast; honor; ply; regale

· ·

The **lissome** yoga instructor twisted herself into shapes that her students could only dream of.

Synonyms: graceful; lithe; supple

· ·

quick, shrewd, and unpredictable

Her **mercurial** personality made it difficult to guess how she would react to the bad news.

Synonyms: clever; crafty; volatile; whimsical

MOTTLE
verb (<u>maht</u> l)

∙∙

MUNIFICENT
adj (myoo <u>nihf</u> ih suhnt)

∙∙

NADIR
noun (<u>nay</u> dihr)

INTERMEDIATE

to mark with spots

Food stains **mottled** the tablecloth.

Synonym: spotted

· ·

generous

The **munificent** millionaire donated ten million dollars to the hospital.

Synonyms: bountiful; liberal

· ·

lowest point

As Lou waited in line to audition for the diaper commercial, he realized he had reached the **nadir** of his acting career.

Synonyms: bottom; depth; pit

NASCENT
adj (<u>nay</u> sehnt)

· ·

NEOPHYTE
noun (<u>nee</u> oh fiet)

· ·

NETTLE
verb (<u>neh</u> tuhl)

INTERMEDIATE

starting to develop, coming into existence

The advertising campaign was still in a **nascent** stage, and nothing had been finalized yet.

Synonyms: embryonic; emerging; inchoate; incipient

• •

novice, beginner

A relative **neophyte** at bowling, Seth rolled all of his balls into the gutter.

Synonyms: apprentice; greenhorn; tyro

• •

to irritate

I don't particularly like having blue hair—I just do it to **nettle** my parents.

Synonyms: annoy; vex

INTERMEDIATE

OBLIQUE
adj (oh bleek)

∙∙∙

OBSEQUIOUS
adj (uhb see kwee uhs)

∙∙∙

OCCLUDE
verb (uh klood)

INTERMEDIATE

indirect, evasive; misleading, devious

Usually open and friendly, Veronica has been behaving in a curiously **oblique** manner lately.

Synonyms: glancing; slanted; tangential

∙∙∙

overly submissive, brownnosing

The **obsequious** new employee complimented her supervisor's tie and agreed with him on every issue.

Synonyms: compliant; fawning; groveling; servile; unctuous

∙∙∙

to shut, block

A shadow is thrown across the Earth's surface during a solar eclipse, when the light from the sun is **occluded** by the moon.

Synonyms: close; obstruct

OFFICIOUS
adj (uh <u>fihsh</u> uhs)

....

ONEROUS
adj (<u>oh</u> neh ruhs)

....

OSTENSIBLE
adj (ah <u>stehn</u> sih buhl)

too helpful, meddlesome

The **officious** waiter butted into the couple's conversation, advising them on how to take out a mortgage.

Synonyms: eager; intrusive; unwanted

● ●

burdensome

The assignment was so difficult to manage that it proved **onerous** to the team in charge of it.

Synonyms: arduous; demanding; exacting; oppressive; rigorous

● ●

apparent

The **ostensible** reason for his visit was to borrow a book, but secretly he wanted to chat with Wanda.

Synonyms: represented; supposed; surface

INTERMEDIATE

OSTENTATIOUS
adj (ah stehn <u>tay</u> shuhs)

· ·

PALL
noun (pawl)

· ·

PALL
verb (pawl)

showy

The billionaire's 200-room palace was considered by many to be an overly **ostentatious** display of wealth.

Synonyms: flamboyant; fulsome; gaudy; ornate; pretentious

. . . .

covering that darkens or obscures; coffin

A **pall** fell over the landscape as the clouds obscured the moon in the night sky.

Synonym: obscurity

. . . .

to lose strength or interest

Over time, the model's beauty **palled,** though her haughty attitude remained intact.

Synonyms: tire; weary

INTERMEDIATE

PARITY
noun (<u>paa</u> ruh tee)

....

PARLEY
noun (<u>pahr</u> lee)

....

PAROCHIAL
adj (puh <u>ro</u> kee uhl)

equality

Mrs. Lutskaya tried to maintain **parity** between her children, although each claimed she gave the other preferential treatment.

Synonyms: equivalence; evenness; par

· ·

discussion, usually between enemies

The peace organization tried in vain to schedule a **parley** between the warring countries.

Synonyms: confabulation; conference

· ·

of limited scope or outlook, provincial

It was obvious that Victor's **parochial** mentality would clash with Ivonne's liberal open-mindedness.

Synonyms: insular; narrow; restricted

PARRY
verb (<u>paa</u> ree)

. . . .

PAUCITY
noun (<u>paw</u> suh tee)

. . . .

PEDAGOGUE
noun (<u>pehd</u> uh gahg)

To ward off or deflect

Kari **parried** every question the interviewer fired at her, much to his frustration.

Synonyms: avoid; evade; repel

· ·

scarcity, lack

Because of the relative **paucity** of bananas in the country, their price was very high.

Synonyms: dearth; deficiency; shortage

· ·

teacher

The beloved professor was known as an influential **pedagogue** at the university.

Synonyn: instructor

PEDANT
noun (<u>peh</u> daant)

....

PERNICIOUS
adj (puhr <u>nih</u> shuhs)

....

PHLEGMATIC
adj (flehg <u>maa</u> tihk)

INTERMEDIATE

uninspired, boring academic

The speaker's tedious commentary on the subject soon gained him a reputation as a **pedant**.

Synonyms: pedagogue; scholar; schoolmaster

• •

very harmful

Poor nutrition and lack of exercise has a **pernicious** effect on the human body.

Synonyms: deadly; destructive; evil; pestilent; wicked

• •

calm in temperament; sluggish

The **phlegmatic** old boar snoozed in the grass as the energetic piglets frolicked around him.

Synonyms: matter-of-fact; undemonstrative

INTERMEDIATE

PLY
verb (plie)

....

PONTIFICATE
verb (pahn <u>tih</u> fih kayt)

....

PRECIPITATE
adj (preh <u>sih</u> puh tayt)

INTERMEDIATE

to join together; to use diligently; to engage

The weaver **plied** the fibers together to make a blanket.

Synonyms: handle; manipulate

● ●

to speak in a pretentious manner

She **pontificated** about the virtues of being rich until we all left the room in disgust.

Synonyms: declaim; lecture; orate; preach; sermonize

● ●

sudden and unexpected

Since the couple wed after knowing each other only a month, many expected their **precipitate** marriage to end in divorce.

Synonyms: abrupt; headlong; impetuous; rash; reckless

INTERMEDIATE

PRECIPITATE
verb (preh <u>sih</u> puh tayt)

··

PRODIGIOUS
adj (pruh <u>dih</u> juhs)

··

PROFLIGATE
adj (<u>praa</u> flih guht)

to cause to happen; to throw down from a height

It's fairly certain that Lloyd's incessant smoking **precipitated** his early death from emphysema.

Synonym: hurl

• •

vast, enormous, extraordinary

The musician's **prodigious** talent made her famous all over the world.

Synonyms: gigantic; huge; impressive; marvelous

• •

corrupt, degenerate

Some historians claim that it was the Romans' decadent, **profligate** behavior that led to the decline of the Roman Empire.

Synonyms: dissolute; extravagant; improvident; prodigal; wasteful

INTERMEDIATE

PROSELYTIZE
verb (prah <u>suhl</u> uh tiez)

· ·

PROTEAN
adj (<u>proh</u> tee uhn)

· ·

PULCHRITUDE
noun (<u>puhl</u> kruh tood)

INTERMEDIATE

to convert to a particular belief or religion

The religious group went from door to door in the neighborhood, **proselytizing** enthusiastically.

Synonyms: convince; missionize; move; preach; sway

· ·

readily assuming different forms or characters

The **protean** actor could play a wide variety of different characters convincingly.

Synonym: versatile

· ·

beauty

The mortals gazed in admiration at Venus, stunned by her incredible **pulchritude**.

Synonyms: comeliness; gorgeousness; handsomeness; loveliness; prettiness

INTERMEDIATE

QUAGMIRE
noun (<u>kwaag</u> mier)

....

QUIXOTIC
adj (kwihk sah tihk)

....

QUOTIDIAN
adj (kwo <u>tih</u> dee uhn)

INTERMEDIATE

marsh; difficult situation

Oliver realized that he needed help to get himself out of this **quagmire**.

Synonyms: bog; fen; mire; morass; swamp

• •

overly idealistic, impractical

The practical Danuta was skeptical of her roommate's **quixotic** plans to build an amphitheater in their yard.

Synonyms: capricious; impulsive; romantic; unrealistic

• •

occurring daily; commonplace

The sight of people singing on the street is so **quotidian** in New York that passersby rarely react to it.

Synonyms: everyday; normal; usual

INTERMEDIATE

RACONTEUR
noun (raa cahn <u>tuhr</u>)

. . . .

RECALCITRANT
adj (ree <u>kaal</u> sih truhnt)

. . . .

REDRESS
noun (<u>rih</u> drehs)

witty, skillful storyteller

The **raconteur** kept all the passengers entertained with his stories during the six-hour flight.

Synonyms: anecdotalist; monologist

• •

resisting authority or control

The **recalcitrant** mule refused to go down the treacherous path, however hard its master pulled at its reins.

Synonyms: defiant; headstrong; stubborn; unruly; willful

• •

relief from wrong or injury

Seeking **redress** for the injuries she had received in the accident, Doreen sued the driver of the truck that had hit her.

Synonyms: amends; indemnity; quittance; reparation; restitution

INTERMEDIATE

REPUDIATE
verb (rih <u>pyoo</u> dee ayt)

· ·

RESTIVE
adj (<u>reh</u> stihv)

· ·

RETRENCH
verb (rih <u>trehnch</u>)

INTERMEDIATE

to reject as having no authority

The old woman's claim that she was Russian royalty was **repudiated** when DNA tests showed she was not related to them.

Synonyms: abjure; disclaim; disown; forswear; renounce

. . . .

impatient, uneasy, restless

The customers became **restive** after having to wait in line for hours, and began to shout complaints at the staff.

Synonyms: agitated; anxious; fretful

. . . .

to cut down; to reduce

The most recent round of layoffs **retrenched** our staff to only three people.

Synonyms: excise; remove; shorten

RIDDLE
verb (<u>rih</u> duhl)

··

SACROSANCT
adj (<u>saa</u> kroh saankt)

··

SARDONIC
adj (sahr <u>dah</u> nihk)

to make many holes in; permeate

The gunfired **riddled** the helicopter with thousands of holes.

Synonyms: honeycomb; perforate; pierce; prick; punch

• •

extremely sacred; beyond criticism

Many people considered Mother Teresa to be **sacrosanct** and would not tolerate any criticism of her.

Synonyms: holy; inviolable; off-limits

• •

cynical, scornfully mocking

Denise was offended by the **sardonic** way in which her date made fun of her ideas and opinions.

Synonyms: acerbic; caustic; sarcastic; satirical; snide

INTERMEDIATE

SCURRILOUS
adj (<u>skuh</u> ruh luhs)

....

SECTARIAN
adj (sehk <u>tayr</u> ee uhn)

....

SENTENTIOUS
adj (sehn <u>tehn</u> shuhs)

INTERMEDIATE

vulgar, low, indecent

The decadent aristocrat took part in **scurrilous** activities every night, unbeknownst to his family.

Synonyms: abusive; coarse; foul-mouthed

. . . .

narrow-minded; relating to a group or sect

Since the fall of Communism in the former Yugoslavia, its various ethnic groups have plunged into **sectarian** violence.

Synonym: schismatic

. . . .

having a moralizing tone

The principal took on a **sententious** tone when he lectured the students on their inappropriate behavior during the school assembly.

Synonyms: aphoristic; moralistic; pithy; pompous; terse

SAT VOCABULARY PREP LEVEL 1

SOMNOLENT
adj (<u>sahm</u> nuh luhnt)

· ·

SONOROUS
adj (sah <u>nuhr</u> uhs)

· ·

SPURIOUS
adj (<u>spyoor</u> ee uhs)

drowsy, sleepy; inducing sleep

Carter became **somnolent** after he ate a huge meal.

Synonyms: sluggish; slumberous; somniferous; soporific

••

producing a full, rich sound

The **sonorous** blaring of the foghorn woke up Lily at 4:30 in the morning.

Synonyms: orotund; resonant; vibrant

••

lacking authenticity; counterfeit, false

Quoting from a **spurious** document, the employee declared that all profits should be signed over to him.

Synonyms: ersatz; fake; fraudulent; mock; phony

INTERMEDIATE

STOLID
adj (<u>stah</u> lihd)

....

SUPERCILIOUS
adj (soo puhr <u>sihl</u> ee uhs)

....

TENABLE
adj (<u>tehn</u> uh buhl)

INTERMEDIATE

having or showing little emotion

The prisoner appeared **stolid** and unaffected by the judge's harsh sentence.

Synonyms: impassive; stoic

• •

arrogant, haughty, overbearing, condescending

She was a shallow and scornful society woman with a **supercilious** manner.

Synonyms: disdainful; patronizing; proud

• •

defensible, reasonable

His decision to quit his job and travel around the world was **tenable** only because he inherited millions of dollars.

Synonyms: maintainable; rational

TUMULT
noun (<u>tuh</u> muhlt)

....

UBIQUITOUS
adj (yoo <u>bihk</u> wih tuhs)

....

UMBRAGE
noun (<u>uhm</u> brihj)

INTERMEDIATE

state of confusion; agitation

The **tumult** of the demonstrators drowned out the police chief's speech.

Synonyms: commotion; chaos; din; disturbance; turmoil

· ·

being everywhere simultaneously

Fast food franchises are **ubiquitous** in the United States, and are common in foreign countries as well.

Synonyms: inescapable; omnipresent

· ·

offense, resentment

The businessman took **umbrage** at the security guard's accusation that he had shoplifted a packet of gum.

Synonyms: asperity; dudgeon; ire; pique; rancor

URBANE
adj (uhr <u>bayn</u>)

· ·

VAUNTED
adj (<u>vawnt</u> ehd)

· ·

VERISIMILITUDE
noun (vehr uh sih <u>mihl</u> ih tood)

INTERMEDIATE

courteous, refined, suave

The **urbane** teenager sneered at the mannerisms of his country-bumpkin cousin.

Synonyms: cosmopolitan; debonair; elegant; polite; soigné

· ·

boasted about, bragged about

The **vaunted** new computer program turned out to have so many bugs that it had to be recalled.

Synonyms: acclaimed; celebrated

· ·

quality of appearing true or real

The TV show's **verisimilitude** led viewers to believe that the characters it portrayed were real.

Synonym: reality

YOKE
verb (yohk)

• •

to join together

As soon as the farmer had **yoked** his oxen together, he began to plow the fields.

Synonyms: bind; harness; pair

••

INTERMEDIATE

ABEYANCE
noun (uh <u>bay</u> uhns)

· ·

ACRIMONY
noun (<u>aak</u> rih moh nee)

· ·

AMELIORATE
verb (uh <u>meel</u> yuhr ayt)

ADVANCED

temporary suppression or suspension

Michelle held her excitement in **abeyance** while the college review board considered her application.

Synonyms: deferral; delay; dormancy; postponement; remission

∙∙

bitterness, animosity

The **acrimony** the newly divorced couple showed towards each other made everyone feel uncomfortable.

Synonyms: antipathy; asperity; choler; rancor; spleen

∙∙

to make better, improve

Conditions in the hospital were **ameliorated** by the hiring of dozens of expertly trained nurses.

Synonyms: amend; better; reform

ADVANCED

ANATHEMA
noun (uh <u>naath</u> uh muh)

....

ANTEDILUVIAN
adj (aan tih duh <u>loo</u> vee uhn)

....

APOCRYPHAL
adj (uh <u>pahk</u> ruh fuhl)

ADVANCED

ban, curse; something shunned or disliked

Sweaty, soiled clothing was **anathema** to the elegant Madeleine.

Synonyms: abomination; aversion; execration; horror

• •

prehistoric, ancient beyond measure

The **antediluvian** fossils were displayed in the museum.

Synonyms: antique; archaic; old

• •

not genuine, fictional

Sharon suspected that the stories she was hearing about alligators in the sewer were **apocryphal**.

Synonyms: erroneous; false; fictitious; fraudulent

ADVANCED

APOTHEOSIS
noun (uh pahth ee <u>oh</u> sihs)
(aap uh <u>thee</u> uh sihs)

....

APPROBATION
noun (aa pruh <u>bay</u> shuhn)

....

ASCETIC
adj (uh <u>seh</u> tihk)

ADVANCED

glorification, glorified ideal

In her heyday, many people considered Jackie Kennedy to be the **apotheosis** of stylishness.

Synonyms: epitome; ultimate

• •

praise, official approval

Billy was sure he had gained the **approbation** of his teacher when he received a glowing report card.

Synonyms: acclaim; accolade; applause; encomium; homage

• •

self-denying, abstinent, austere

The monk lived an **ascetic** life deep in the wilderness, denying himself all forms of luxury.

Synonyms: abstemious; continent; temperate

ASPERSION
noun (uh <u>spuhr</u> shuhn)

. . . .

ATTENUATE
verb (uh <u>tehn</u> yoo ayt)

. . . .

AUGURY
noun (<u>aw</u> gyuh ree) (<u>aw</u> guh ree)

ADVANCED

false rumor, damaging report, slander

It is unfair to cast **aspersions** on someone behind his or her back.

Synonyms: allegation; insinuation; reproach

• •

to make thin or slender; to weaken

The Bill of Rights **attenuated** the traditional power of government to change laws at will.

Synonyms: diminish; raregy; reduce

• •

prophecy, prediction of events

Troy hoped the rainbow was an **augury** of good things to come.

Synonyms: auspices; harbinger; omen; portent; presage

AXIOM
noun (<u>aak</u> see uhm)

· ·

BELLICOSE
adj (<u>beh</u> lih cohs)

· ·

BENIGHTED
adj (bih <u>nie</u> tihd)

ADVANCED

premise, postulate, self-evident truth

Halle lived her life based on the **axioms** her grandmother had passed on to her.

Synonyms: adage; aphorism; apothegm; maxim; rule

· ·

warlike, aggressive

Immediately after defeating one of his enemies, the **bellicose** chieftain declared war on another.

Synonyms: belligerent; combative; hostile; pugnacious

· ·

unenlightened

Ben scoffed at the crowd, as he believed it consisted entirely of **benighted** individuals.

Synonyms: ignorant; illiterate; unschooled

BONHOMIE
noun (bahn uh <u>mee</u>)

....

BRIGAND
noun (<u>brihg</u> uhnd)

....

CAPACIOUS
adj (kuh <u>pay</u> shuhs)

good-natured geniality; atmosphere of good cheer

The general **bonhomie** that characterized the party made it a joy to attend.

Synonym: friendliness

••

bandit, outlaw

Brigands held up the bank and made off with the contents of the safe.

Synonym: plunderer

••

large, roomy; extensive

We wondered how many hundreds of stores occupied the **capacious** mall.

Synonyms: ample; commodious

ADVANCED

CAPITULATE
verb (kuh <u>pih</u> choo layt)

. . . .

CASTIGATE
verb (<u>kaa</u> stih gayt)

. . . .

CHICANERY
noun (shih <u>kayn</u> ree) (shi <u>kay</u> nuh ree)
("ch" can replace "sh")

to submit completely, surrender

After the army was reduced to only five soldiers, there was little choice but to **capitulate**.

Synonyms: acquiesce; succumb; yield

· ·

to punish, chastise, criticize severely

Authorities in Singapore harshly **castigate** perpetrators of what would be considered minor crimes in the United States.

Synonyms: discipline; lambaste

· ·

trickery, fraud, deception

Dishonest used car salesmen often use **chicanery** to sell their beat-up old cars.

Synonyms: deceit; dishonesty; duplicity

ADVANCED

CIRCUMLOCUTION
noun (suhr kuhm loh <u>kyoo</u> shuhn)

· ·

COALESCE
verb (koh uh <u>lehs</u>)

· ·

COLLUSION
noun (kuh <u>loo</u> zhuhn)

roundabout, lengthy way of saying something

He avoided discussing the real issues with endless **circumlocution**.

Synonyms: evasion; wordiness

• •

to grow together or cause to unite as one

The different factions of the organization **coalesced** to form one united front against their opponents.

Synonyms: combine; merge

• •

collaboration, complicity, conspiracy

The teacher realized that the students were in **collusion** when everyone received the same grade on the test.

Synonyms: connivance; intrigue; machination

COMMODIOUS
adj (kuh <u>moh</u> dee uhs)

··

COMPLICITY
noun (kuhm <u>plih</u> sih tee)

··

CONCILIATORY
adj (kuhn <u>sihl</u> ee uh tohr ee)

roomy, spacious

Raqiyah was able to stretch out fully in the **commodious** bathtub.

Synonyms: ample; capacious; extensive

• •

knowing partnership in wrongdoing

The two boys exchanged a look of sly **complicity** when their father shouted "Who broke the window?"

Synonyms: cahoots; collaboration; involvement

• •

overcoming distrust or hostility

Fred made the **conciliatory** gesture of buying Abby flowers after their big fight.

Synonym: pleasing

CONTRAVENE
verb (kahn truh <u>veen</u>)

· ·

CORPOREAL
adj (kohr <u>pohr</u> ee uhl)

· ·

COSSET
verb (<u>kahs</u> iht)

ADVANCED

to contradict, deny, act contrary to

The watchman **contravened** his official instructions by leaving his post for an hour.

Synonyms: disobey; transgress; violate

• •

having to do with the body; tangible, material

Makiko realized that the problem was **corporeal** in nature; it was not just an intangible issue.

Synonyms: concrete; physical; somatic

• •

to pamper, treat with great care

Mimi **cosseted** her toy poodle, feeding it gourmet meals and buying it a silk pillow to sleep on.

Synonym: spoil

ADVANCED

COUNTENANCE
verb (<u>kown</u> tuh nuhns)

· ·

COUNTERMAND
verb (<u>kown</u> tuhr maand)

· ·

CUPIDITY
noun (kyoo <u>pih</u> dih tee)

ADVANCED

to favor, support

When the girls started a pillow fight, the baby-sitter warned them, "I will not **countenance** such behavior."

Synonyms: approve; tolerate

. . . .

to annul, cancel, make a contrary order

Residents were relieved when the councilmembers **countermanded** the rule of 30-minute parking on all city streets.

Synonym: revoke

. . . .

greed

The poverty-stricken man stared at the shining jewels with **cupidity** in his gleaming eyes.

Synonyms: avarice; covetousness; rapacity

ADVANCED

DECLIVITY
noun (dih <u>klih</u> vih tee)

· ·

DEMUR
verb (dih <u>muhr</u>)

· ·

DEROGATE
verb (<u>dehr</u> uh gayt)

downward slope

Because the village was situated on the **declivity** of a hill, it never flooded.

Synonyms: decline; descent; grade; slant; tilt

. . . .

to express doubts or objections

When scientific authorities claimed that all the planets revolved around the Earth, Galileo, with his superior understanding of the situation, was forced to **demur**.

Synonyms: expostulate; dissent; kick; protest, remonstrate

. . . .

to belittle; to disparage

The sarcastic old man never stopped **derogating** the efforts of his daughter, even after she won the Nobel Prize.

Synonym: detract

DESICCATE
verb (<u>deh</u> sih kayt)

· ·

DESULTORY
adj (<u>dehs</u> uhl tohr ee) (<u>dehz</u> uhl tohr ee)

· ·

DICTUM
noun (<u>dihk</u> tuhm)

ADVANCED

to dry completely, dehydrate

The hot desert sun will **desiccate** anyone who dares spend the day there without any source of water.

Synonyms: evaporate; exsiccate; parch

. . . .

at random, rambling, unmethodical

Diane had a **desultory** academic record; she had changed majors 12 times in three years.

Synonym: chaotic

. . . .

authoritative statement; popular saying

Chris tried to live his life in accordance with the **dictum** "Two wrongs don't make a right."

Synonyms: adage; aphorism; apothegm; decree; edict

DIFFIDENCE
noun (<u>dih</u> fih duhns) (<u>dih</u> fih dehns)

. . . .

DILATORY
adj (<u>dihl</u> uh tohr ee)

. . . .

DISCURSIVE
adj (dih <u>skuhr</u> sihv)

ADVANCED

shyness, lack of confidence

Steve's **diffidence** during the job interview stemmed from his nervous nature and lack of experience.

Synonyms: reticence; timidity

· ·

slow, tending to delay

The congressman used **dilatory** measures to delay the passage of the bill.

Synonyms: sluggish; tardy; unhurried

· ·

wandering from topic to topic

The professor, known for his **discursive** speaking style, covered everything from armadillos to zebras in his zoology lecture.

Synonym: rambling

ADVANCED

DISSEMBLE
verb (dihs <u>sehm</u> buhl)

....

DITHER
verb (<u>dihth</u> uhr)

....

DIURNAL
adj (die <u>uhr</u> nuhl)

to pretend, disguise one's motives

The villain could **dissemble** to the lawyers no longer—he finally had to confess to the forgery.

Synonyms: camouflage; cloak; conceal; feign

• •

to move or act confusedly or without clear purpose

Ellen **dithered** around her apartment, uncertain how to tackle the family crisis.

Synonyms: falter; hesitate; vacillate; waffle; waver

• •

daily

Diurnal creatures tend to become inactive during the night.

Synonyms: daylight, daytime

ADVANCED

DOGMATIC
adj (dahg <u>maat</u> ihk) (dawg <u>maat</u> ihk)

· ·

DYSPEPTIC
adj (dihs <u>pehp</u> tihk)

· ·

EFFACE
verb (ih <u>fays</u>) (eh <u>fays</u>)

rigidly fixed in opinion, opinionated

The dictator was **dogmatic**—he, and only he, was right.

Synonyms: authoritative; doctrinaire; inflexible; obstinate

· ·

suffering from indigestion; gloomy and irritable

The **dyspeptic** young man cast a gloom over the party the minute he walked in.

Synonyms: melancholy; morose; solemn; sour

· ·

to erase or make illegible

Benjamin attempted to **efface** all traces of his troubled past by assuming a completely new identity.

Synonyms: expunge; obliterate

EFFICACIOUS
adj (eff uh <u>kay</u> shuhs)

· ·

EFFRONTERY
noun (ih <u>fruhnt</u> uhr ee) (eh <u>fruhnt</u> uhr ee)

· ·

EFFULGENT
adj (ih <u>fool</u> juhnt) (ih <u>fuhl</u> juhnt)

ADVANCED

effective, efficient

Penicillin was one of the most **efficacious** drugs on the market when it was first introduced; the drug completely eliminated almost all bacterial infections for which it was administered.

Synonyms: effectual; potent

• •

impudent boldness; audacity

The receptionist had the **effrontery** to laugh out loud when her boss tripped over a computer wire and fell flat on his face.

Synonyms: brashness; gall; nerve; presumption; temerity

• •

brilliantly shining

The **effulgent** stars that filled the dark evening sky dazzled the sharecroppers.

Synonym: glowing

ADVANCED

ELUCIDATE
verb (ih <u>loo</u> suh dayt)

· ·

ENDEMIC
adj (ehn <u>deh</u> mihk)

· ·

ENERVATE
verb (<u>ehn</u> uhr vayt)

to explain, clarify

The teacher **elucidated** the reasons why she had failed the student to his upset parents.

Synonyms: define; explicate; illuminate; interpret

. . . .

belonging to a particular area, inherent

The health department determined that the outbreak was **endemic** to the small village, so they quarantined the inhabitants before the virus could spread.

Synonyms: indigenous; local; native

. . . .

to weaken, sap strength from

The guerrillas hoped that a series of surprise attacks would **enervate** the regular army.

Synonyms: debilitate; deplete; drain; exhaust

ADVANCED

ENNUI
noun (ahn <u>wee</u>) (<u>ahn</u> wee)

....

EPICURE
noun (<u>eh</u> pih kyoor) (<u>eh</u> pih kyuhr)

....

EPIGRAM
noun (<u>eh</u> puh graam)

ADVANCED

boredom, lack of interest and energy

Joe tried to alleviate the **ennui** he felt while doing his tedious job by shopping online.

Synonyms: listlessness; tedium; world-weariness

· ·

a person with refined taste in cuisine

Restaurant critics should be **epicures,** as people rely on their judgments in choosing where to eat.

Synonyms: connoisseur; gastronome; gourmand; gourmet

· ·

short, witty saying or poem

The poet was renowned for his skill in making up amusing **epigrams**.

Synonyms: adage; aphorism; maxim; saw

EQUANIMITY
noun (ee kwuh <u>nihm</u> ih tee)
(ehk wuh <u>nihm</u> ih tee)

· ·

ERUDITE
adj (<u>ehr</u> yuh diet) (<u>ehr</u> uh diet)

· ·

ETHOS
noun (<u>ee</u> thohs)

calmness, composure

Kelly took the news that she had been fired with outward **equanimity**, though she was crying inside.

Synonyms: aplomb; coolness; poise; sang-froid; serenity

• •

learned, scholarly

The annual meeting of professors brought together the most **erudite** individuals in the field.

Synonyms: cultured; educated; knowledgeable; literate; well-read

• •

beliefs or character of a group

In accordance with the **ethos** of his people, the man completed the tasks that would allow him to become the new chief.

Synonym: sentiment

EVANESCENT
adj (eh vuh <u>nehs</u> uhnt)

· ·

EVINCE
verb (ih <u>vihns</u>)

· ·

EXECRABLE
adj (<u>ehk</u> sih kruh buhl)

ADVANCED

momentary, transitory, short-lived

It is lucky that solar eclipses are **evanescent,** or the world would never see sunlight.

Synonyms: ephemeral; fleeting; fugitive; transient

• •

to show clearly, display, signify

The new secretary **evinced** impressive typing and filing skills.

Synonym: demonstrate

• •

utterly detestable, abhorrent

The stew tasted **execrable** after the cook accidentally dumped a pound of salt into it.

Synonyms: awful; hateful; horrible; inferior; terrible

EXPIATE
verb (<u>ehk</u> spee ayt)

....

EXPURGATE
verb (<u>ehk</u> spuhr gayt)

....

FLORID
adj (<u>flohr</u> ihd) (<u>flahr</u> ihd)

to atone for, make amends for

The nun **expiated** her sins by scrubbing the floor of the convent on her hands and knees.

Synonyms: answer; compensate; pay

• •

to censor

Government propagandists **expurgated** all negative references to the dictator from the film.

Synonyms: bowdlerize; cut; sanitize

• •

gaudy, extremely ornate; ruddy, flushed

The palace had been decorated in an excessively **florid** style; every surface had been carved and gilded.

Synonyms: flamboyant; garish; loud; ornate; ostentatious

ADVANCED

FOMENT
verb (foh <u>mehnt</u>)

. . . .

FULSOME
adj (<u>fool</u> suhm)

. . . .

GAMBOL
verb (<u>gaam</u> buhl)

ADVANCED

to arouse or incite

The protesters tried to **foment** feeling against the war through their speeches and demonstrations.

Synonyms: abet; instigate; promote

· ·

sickeningly excessive; repulsive

Diana felt nauseous at the sight of the rich, **fulsome** dishes weighing down the table at the banquet.

Synonyms: copious; overdone

· ·

to dance or skip around playfully

The parents gathered to watch the children **gambol** about the yard.

Synonym: frolic

GIBE
verb (jieb)

. . . .

GUSTATORY
adj (<u>goos</u> tuh tohr ee)

. . . .

HACKNEYED
adj (<u>haak</u> need)

to make heckling, taunting remarks

Tina **gibed** at her brothers mercilessly as they clumsily attempted to pitch the tent.

Synonyms: deride; jeer; mock; ridicule; twit

· ·

relating to sense of taste

Murdock claimed that he loved cooking because he enjoyed the **gustatory** pleasures in life.

Synonym: culinary

· ·

worn out by overuse

We always mock my father for his **hackneyed** expressions and dated hairstyle.

Synonyms: banal; shopworn; stale; trite

ADVANCED

HIDEBOUND
adj (<u>hied</u> bownd)

· ·

HOARY
adj (<u>hohr</u> ee) (<u>haw</u> ree)

· ·

IGNOMINIOUS
adj (ihg nuh <u>mih</u> nee uhs)

ADVANCED

excessively rigid; dry and stiff

The **hidebound** old patriarch would not tolerate any opposition to his orders.

Synonyms: conservative; inflexible

• •

very old; whitish or gray from age

The old man's **hoary** beard contrasted starkly to the new stubble of his teenage grandson.

Synonyms: ancient; antediluvian; antique; vernerable; vintage

• •

disgraceful and dishonorable

He was humiliated by his **ignominious** dismissal.

Synonyms: debasing; degrading; despicable

ADVANCED

IMPECUNIOUS
adj (ihm pih <u>kyoo</u> nyuhs)
(ihm pih <u>kyoo</u> nee uhs)

....

IMPORTUNE
verb (ihm pohr <u>toon</u>) (ihm <u>pohr</u> chuhn)

....

IMPROVIDENT
adj (ihm <u>prahv</u> ih duhnt)

ADVANCED

poor, having no money

After the crash of thousands of tech startups, many Internet millionaires found themselves **impecunious**.

Synonyms: destitute; impoverished; indigent; needy; penniless

••

to ask repeatedly, beg

The assistant **importuned** her boss with constant requests for a raise and promotion.

Synonyms: annoy; trouble

••

without planning or foresight, negligent

The **improvident** woman spent all the money she received in her court settlement within two weeks.

Synonym: unprepared

ADVANCED

INCHOATE
adj (ihn <u>koh</u> iht)

· ·

INCIPIENT
adj (ihn <u>sihp</u> ee uhnt)

· ·

INCULCATE
verb (ihn <u>kuhl</u> kayt) (<u>ihn</u> kuhl kayt)

imperfectly formed or formulated

As her thoughts on the subject were still in **inchoate** form, Amalia could not explain what she meant.

Synonyms: formless; undefined

• •

beginning to exist or appear; in an initial stage

At that point, her financial problems were only **incipient** and she could still pay her bills.

Synonyms: basic; developing

• •

to teach, impress in the mind

Most parents blithely **inculcate** their children with their political views instead of allowing their children to select their own.

Synonyms: implant; indoctrinate; instill; preach

INCULPATE
verb (ihn <u>kuhl</u> payt) (ihn <u>kuhl</u> payt)

....

INDUBITABLE
adj (ihn <u>doo</u> bih tuh buhl)
(ihn <u>dyoo</u> bih tuh buhl)

....

INEXORABLE
adj (ihn <u>ehk</u> suhr uh buhl)

ADVANCED

to blame, charge with a crime

His suspicious behavior after the break-in led authorities to **inculpate** him.

Synonym: incriminate

· ·

unquestionable

His **indubitable** cooking skills made it all the more astonishing when the Thanksgiving dinner he prepared tasted awful.

Synonyms: apparent; certain; unassailable

· ·

inflexible, unyielding

The **inexorable** force of the tornado swept away their house.

Synonyms: adamant; obdurate; relentless

INGENUOUS
adj (ihn <u>jehn</u> yoo uhs)

· ·

INGRESS
noun (<u>ihn</u> grehs)

· ·

INIMICAL
adj (ih <u>nihm</u> ih kuhl)

ADVANCED

straightforward, open; naive and unsophisticated

She was so **ingenuous** that her friends feared that her innocence would be exploited when she visited the big city.

Synonyms: artless; candid; natural; simple; unaffected

•••

entrance

Ed hoped that the mailroom job would provide him with an **ingress** into the company.

Synonym: entry

•••

hostile, unfriendly

Even though a cease-fire had been in place for months, the two sides were still **inimical** to each other.

Synonyms: adverse; antagonistice; harmful; injurious

INTERPOLATE
verb (ihn <u>tuhr</u> puh layt)

. . . .

INTRANSIGENT
adj (ihn <u>traan</u> suh juhnt)
(ihn <u>traan</u> zuh juhnt)

. . . .

INURE
verb (ihn <u>yoor</u>)

to insert; to change by adding new words or material

The editor **interpolated** a few new sentences into the manuscript, and the new edition was ready to print.

Synonym: intercalate

• •

uncompromising, refusing to be reconciled

The professor was **intransigent** on the deadline, insisting that everyone turn the assignment in on Friday.

Synonyms: obstinate; unyielding

• •

to harden; to accustom; to become used to

Eventually, Hassad became **inured** to the sirens that went off every night and could sleep through them.

Synonyms: condition; familiarize; habituate

INVECTIVE
noun (ihn <u>vehk</u> tihv)

....

INVIDIOUS
adj (ihn <u>vihd</u> ee uhs)

....

JINGOISM
noun (<u>jing</u> goh ihz uhm)

ADVANCED

verbal abuse

A stream of **invective** poured from Mrs. Pratt's mouth as she watched the vandals smash her ceramic frog.

Synonyms: denunciation; revilement; vituperation

• •

envious; obnoxious

It is cruel and **invidious** for parents to play favorites with their children.

Synonyms: discriminatory; insulting; jaundiced; resentful

• •

belligerent support of one's country

The president's **jingoism** made him declare war on other countries at the slightest provocation.

Synonyms: chauvinism; nationalism

JURISPRUDENCE
noun (joor his <u>prood</u> ns)

. . . .

LACHRYMOSE
adj (<u>laak</u> ruh mohs)

. . . .

LEGERDEMAIN
noun (lehj uhr duh <u>mayn</u>)

ADVANCED

philosophy of law

An expert in **jurisprudence,** the esteemed lawyer was often consulted by his colleagues.

Synonym: legal matters

· ·

tearful

Heather always became **lachrymose** when it was time to bid her daughter good-bye.

Synonyms: teary; weepy

· ·

trickery

The magician was skilled in the arts of **legerdemain.**

Synonym: adroitness

ADVANCED

LUGUBRIOUS
adj (loo <u>goo</u> bree uhs)

• •

MALADROIT
adj (maal uh <u>droyt</u>)

• •

MALINGER
verb (muh <u>ling</u> guhr)

ADVANCED

sorrowful, mournful; dismal

Irish wakes are a rousing departure from the **lugubrious** funeral services most people are accustomed to.

Synonyms: funereal; gloomy; melancholy; somber; woeful

• •

clumsy, tactless

His **maladroit** comments about the host's poor cooking skills were viewed as inexcusable by the other guests.

Synonyms: awkward; gauche; inept; ungainly

• •

to evade responsibility by pretending to be ill

A common way to dodge the draft was by **malingering**—faking an illness so as to avoid having to serve in the Army.

Synonyms: fake, shirk

ADVANCED

MARTINET
noun (mahr tihn <u>eht</u>)

....

MENDACIOUS
adj (mehn <u>day</u> shuhs)

....

MENDICANT
noun (<u>mehn</u> dih kuhnt)

strict disciplinarian, one who rigidly follows rules

A complete **martinet**, the official insisted that Pete fill out all the forms again even though he was already familiar with his case.

Synonyms: dictator, stickler; tyrant

• •

dishonest

So many of her stories were **mendacious** that I decided she must be a pathological liar.

Synonyms: deceitful; false; lying; untruthful

• •

beggar

"Please, sir, can you spare a dime?" begged the **mendicant** as the businessman walked past.

Synonyms: panhandler; pauper

MILITATE
verb (<u>mihl</u> ih tayt)

· ·

MORIBUND
adj (<u>mohr</u> uh buhnd)

· ·

MULTIFARIOUS
adj (muhl tuh <u>faar</u> ee uhs)

to operate against, work against

The unprofessional employee **militated** against his supervisor, without realizing the ramifications of his actions.

Synonyms: affect; change; influence

• •

dying, decaying

Thanks to the feminist movement, many sexist customs are now **moribund** in this society.

Synonyms: deceasing; succumbing

• •

diverse

Ken opened the hotel room window, letting in the **multifarious** noises of the great city.

Synonym: various

NOISOME
adj (<u>noy</u> suhm)

....

OBSTREPEROUS
adj (<u>ahb</u> strehp uhr uhs)
(<u>uhb</u> strehp uhr uhs)

....

OBVIATE
verb (<u>ahb</u> vee ayt)

ADVANCED

stinking, putrid

A dead mouse trapped in your walls produces a **noisome** odor.

Synonyms: disgusting; foul; malodorous

• •

troublesome, boisterous, unruly

The **obstreperous** toddler, who was always breaking things, was the terror of his nursery school.

Synonym: vociferous

• •

to make unnecessary; to anticipate and prevent

The river was shallow enough for the riders to wade across, which **obviated** the need for a bridge.

Synonyms: avert; deter; forestall; preclude

PALAVER
noun (puh <u>laav</u> uhr) (puh <u>lah</u> vuhr)

· ·

PALLIATE
verb (<u>paa</u> lee ayt)

· ·

PANACEA
noun (paan uh <u>see</u> uh)

ADVANCED

idle talk

The journalist eagerly recorded the **palaver** among the football players in the locker room.

Synonym: chit-chat

. . . .

to make less serious, ease

The accused's crime was so vicious that the defense lawyer could not **palliate** it for the jury.

Synonyms: alleviate; assuage; extenuate; mitigate

. . . .

cure-all

Some claim that vitamin C is a **panacea** for all sorts of illnesses, but I have my doubts.

Synonyms: elixir; miracle drug; sovereign remedy

ADVANCED

PANOPLY
noun (<u>paan</u> uh plee)

· ·

PARSIMONY
noun (<u>pahr</u> sih moh nee)

· ·

PASTICHE
noun (pah <u>steesh</u>)

ADVANCED

impressive array

Corrina casually sifted through a **panoply** of job offers before finally deciding on one.

Synonym: large variety

• •

stinginess

Ethel gained a reputation for **parsimony** when she refused to pay for her daughter's college education.

Synonyms: economy; frugality; meanness; miserliness

• •

piece of literature or music imitating other works

The playwright's clever **pastiche** of the well-known fairy tale had the audience rolling in the aisles.

Synonyms: medley; spoof

ADVANCED

PECCADILLO
noun (pehk uh <u>dih</u> loh)

....

PEJORATIVE
noun (<u>peh</u> jaw ruh tihv)

....

PERCIPIENT
adj (puhr <u>sihp</u> ee uhnt)

ADVANCED

minor sin or offense

Gabriel tends to harp on his brother's **peccadilloes** and never lets him live them down.

Synonyms: failing; fault; lapse; misstep

· ·

having bad connotations; disparaging

The teacher scolded Mark for his unduly **pejorative** comments about his classmate's presentation.

Synonyms: belittling; dismissive; insulting

· ·

discerning, able to perceive

The **percipient** detective saw through the suspect's lies and uncovered the truth in the matter.

Synonyms: insightful; perceptive

ADVANCED

PERFIDIOUS
adj (puhr <u>fih</u> dee uhs)

....

PERIPATETIC
adj (peh ruh puh <u>teh</u> tihk)

....

PERSPICACIOUS
adj (puhr spuh <u>kay</u> shuhs)

faithless, disloyal, untrustworthy

The actress's **perfidious** companion revealed all of her intimate secrets to the gossip columnist.

Synonyms: deceitful; devious; treacherous

· ·

moving from place to place

Morty claims that his **peripatetic** hot dog stand gives him the opportunity to travel all over the city.

Synonyms: itinerant; nomadic; vagabond

· ·

shrewd, astute, keen witted

Inspector Poirot used his **perspicacious** mind to solve mysteries.

Synonyms: insightful; intelligent; sagacious

PERTINACIOUS
adj (puhr tn <u>ay</u> shuhs)

· ·

POLEMIC
noun (puh <u>leh</u> mihk)

· ·

PRESCIENT
adj (<u>preh</u> shuhnt)

ADVANCED

persistent, stubborn

Despite her parents' opposition, Tina was **pertinacious** in her insistence to travel alone.

Synonym: obstitnate

• •

controversy, argument; verbal attack

The candidate's **polemic** against his opponent was vicious and small-minded rather than well reasoned and convincing.

Synonyms: denunciation; refutation

• •

having foresight

Jonah's decision to sell the apartment turned out to be a **prescient** one, as its value soon dropped by half.

Synonyms: augural; divinatory; mantic; oracular; premonitory

PREVARICATE
verb (prih <u>vaar</u> uh cayt)

....

PRIVATION
noun (prih <u>vay</u> shuhn)

....

PROBITY
noun (<u>proh</u> buh tee)

to lie, evade the truth

Rather than admit that he had overslept again, the employee **prevaricated**, claiming that traffic had made him late.

Synonyms: equivocate; fabricate; fib; hedge; palter

· ·

lack of usual necessities or comforts

The convict endured total **privation** while locked up in solitary confinement for a month.

Synonyms: deprivation; forfeiture; loss; poverty

· ·

honesty, high-mindedness

The conscientious witness responded with the utmost **probity** to all the questions posed to her.

Synonyms: honor; integrity; rectitude; uprightness; virtue

ADVANCED

PROPINQUITY
noun (pruh <u>pihng</u> kwih tee)

....

PROPITIOUS
adj (pruh <u>pih</u> shuhs)

....

QUERULOUS
adj (<u>kwehr</u> yoo luhs)

ADVANCED

ADVANCED

nearness

The house's **propinquity** to the foul-smelling pig farm made it impossible to sell.

Synonym: proximity

· ·

favorable, advantageous

"I realize that I should have brought this up at a more **propitious** moment, but I don't love you," said the bride to the groom in the middle of their marriage vows.

Synonyms: auspicious; benign; conducive

· ·

inclined to complain, irritable

Curtis's complaint letter received prompt attention after the company labeled him a **querulous** customer.

Synonyms: peevish; puling; whiny; sniveling

QUIESCENCE
noun (kwie <u>eh</u> sihns)

....

RECONDITE
adj (<u>rehk</u> uhn diet) (rih <u>kahn</u> diet)

....

RECTITUDE
noun (<u>rehk</u> tih tood)

ADVANCED

inactivity, stillness

Bears typically fall into a state of **quiescence** when they hibernate during the winter months.

Synonyms: calm; dormancy; idleness; repose

• •

relating to obscure learning; known to only a few

The ideas expressed in the ancient philosophical treatise were so **recondite** that only a few scholars could appreciate them.

Synonym: esoteric

• •

moral uprightness

Young women used to be shipped off to finishing schools to teach them proper manners and **rectitude**.

Synonyms: honesty; honor; integrity; probity; righteousness

ADVANCED

REJOINDER
noun (rih <u>joyn</u> duhr)

....

REPROBATE
noun (reh <u>pruh</u> bayt)

....

RETINUE
noun (<u>reht</u> noo)

response

Patrick tried desperately to think of a clever **rejoinder** to Marcy's joke, but he couldn't.

Synonyms: retort; riposte

• •

morally unprincipled person

If you ignore your society's accepted moral code, you will be considered a **reprobate**.

Synonyms: knave; rake; rogue; scoundrel; sinner

• •

group of attendants with an important person

The nobleman had to make room in his mansion not only for the princess, but also for her entire **retinue**.

Synonyms: entourage; following

ADVANCED

SAGACIOUS
adj (suh <u>gay</u> shuhs)

· ·

SALUBRIOUS
adj (suh <u>loo</u> bree uhs)

· ·

SANGUINE
adj (<u>saan</u> gwuhn)

ADVANCED

shrewd

Owls have a reputation for being **sagacious**, perhaps because of their big eyes which resemble glasses.

Synonyms: astute; judicious; perspicacious; sage; wise

• •

healthful

Rundown and sickly, Rita hoped that the fresh mountain air would have a **salubrious** effect on her health.

Synonyms: bracing; curative; medicinal; therapeutic; tonic

• •

ruddy; cheerfully optimistic

A **sanguine** person thinks the glass is half full, while a depressed person thinks it's half empty.

Synonyms: confident; hopeful; positive; rosy; rubicund

ADVANCED

SCINTILLA
noun (sihn <u>tihl</u> uh)

· ·

SCINTILLATE
verb (<u>sihn</u> tuhl ayt)

· ·

SENESCENT
adj (sih <u>nehs</u> uhnt)

ADVANCED

trace amount

This poison is so powerful that no more of a **scintilla** of it is needed to kill a horse.

Synonyms: atom; iota; mote; spark; speck

• •

to sparkle, flash

The society hostess was famous for throwing parties that **scintillated** and impressed every guest.

Synonyms: gleam; glisten; glitter; shimmer; twinkle

• •

aging, growing old

Fearful of becoming **senescent**, Jobim worked out several times a week and ate only healthy foods.

Synonyms: aged; mature

ADVANCED

SOLECISM
noun (<u>sahl</u> ih sihz uhm)
(<u>sohl</u> ih sihz uhm)

· ·

SOLIPSISM
noun (<u>sahl</u> ihp sihz uhm)
(<u>sohl</u> ihp sihz uhm)

· ·

SOPHISTRY
noun (<u>sahf</u> ih stree)

ADVANCED

grammatical mistake

The applicant's letter was filled with embarrassing **solecisms,** such as "I works here at 20 years."

Synonym: language blunder

· ·

belief that oneself is the only reality

Arthur's **solipsism** annoyed others, since he treated them as if they didn't exist.

Synonym: self-interest

· ·

deceptive reasoning or argumentation

The politician used **sophistry** to cloud the issue whenever he was asked a tough question in a debate.

Synonym: cogitation

ADVANCED

SOPORIFIC
adj (sahp uhr <u>ihf</u> ihk)

. . . .

STULTIFY
verb (<u>stuhl</u> tuh fie)

. . . .

SUBJUGATE
verb (<u>suhb</u> juh gayt)

ADVANCED

sleepy or tending to cause sleep

The movie proved to be so **soporific** that soon loud snores were heard throughout the theater.

Synonyms: drowsy; narcotic; somniferous; somnolent

· ·

to impair or reduce to uselessness

The company's leadership was **stultified** by its practice of promoting the owner's incapable children to powerful positions.

Synonyms: damage; mar

· ·

to conquer, subdue; to enslave

The Romans **subjugated** all the peoples they conquered, often enslaving them.

Synonyms: defeat; enthrall; vanquish; yoke

ADVANCED

SUPERANNUATED
adj (soo puhr <u>aan</u> yoo ay tihd)

· ·

SURFEIT
noun (<u>suhr</u> fiht)

· ·

TIMOROUS
adj (<u>tih</u> muhr uhs)

ADVANCED

too old, obsolete, outdated

The manual typewriter has become **superannuated**, although a few loyal diehards still swear by it.

Synonyms: disused; outworn

• •

excessive amount

Because of the **surfeit** of pigs, pork prices have never been lower.

Synonyms: glut; plethora; repletion; superfluity; surplus

• •

timid, shy, full of apprehension

A **timorous** woman, Lois relied on her children to act for her whenever aggressive behavior was called for.

Synonyms: anxious; fearful; frightened

TORPID
adj (<u>tohr</u> pihd)

··

TRACTABLE
adj (<u>traak</u> tuh buhl)

··

TRENCHANT
adj (<u>trehn</u> chuhnt)

lethargic; unable to move; dormant

After surgery, the patient was **torpid** until the anesthesia wore off.

Synonyms: apathetic; benumbed; hibernating; inactive; inert

· ·

obedient, yielding

Though it was exhausted, the **tractable** workhorse obediently dragged the carriage through the mud.

Synonyms: acquiescent; compliant; docile; governable; malleable

· ·

acute, sharp, incisive; forceful, effective

Dan's **trenchant** observations in class made him the professor's favorite student.

Synonyms: biting; caustic; cutting; keen

TYRO
noun (<u>tie</u> roh)

· ·

UNCTUOUS
adj (<u>ungk</u> choo uhs)

· ·

UPBRAID
verb (uhp <u>brayd</u>)

ADVANCED

beginner, novice

An obvious **tyro** at salsa, Millicent received no invitations to dance.

Synonyms: apprentice; fledgling; greenhorn; neophyte; tenderfoot

· ·

greasy, oily; smug and falsely earnest

The **unctuous** salesman showered the rich customers with exaggerated compliments.

Synonyms: fulsome; phony; smarmy

· ·

to scold sharply

The teacher **upbraided** the student for scrawling graffiti all over the walls of the school.

Synonyms: berate; chide; reproach; rebuke; tax

ADVANCED

VICISSITUDE
noun (vih <u>sih</u> sih tood)

....

VENERATE
verb (<u>vehn</u> uhr ayt)

....

VERDANT
adj (<u>vuhr</u> dnt)

change or variation; ups and downs

Investors must be prepared for **vicissitudes** in the market and not panic when stock prices fall occasionally.

Synonyms: inconstancy; mutability

• •

to adore, honor, respect

In traditional Confucian society, the young **venerate** the older members of their village, and defer to the elders' wisdom.

Synonym: regard

• •

green with vegetation; inexperienced

He wandered deep into the **verdant** woods in search of mushrooms and other edible flora.

Synonyms: grassy; leafy; wooded

ADVANCED

SAT ROOT LIST

A, AN—not, without
AB, A—from, away, apart
AC, ACR—sharp, sour
AD, A—to, towards
ALI, ALTR—another
AM, AMI—love
AMBI, AMPHI—both
AMBL, AMBUL—walk
ANIM—mind, spirit, breath
ANN, ENN—year
ANTE, ANT—before
ANTHROP—human
ANTI, ANT—against, opposite
AUD—hear
AUTO—self
BELLI, BELL—war
BENE, BEN—good
BI—two
BIBLIO—book
BIO—life
BURS—money, purse
CAD, CAS, CID—happen, fall
CAP, CIP—head
CARN—flesh

CAP, CAPT, CEPT, CIP—take,
    hold, seize
CED, CESS—yield, go
CHROM—color
CHRON—time
CIDE—murder
CIRCUM—around
CLIN, CLIV—slope
CLUD, CLUS, CLAUS, CLOIS—
    shut, close
CO, COM, CON—with,
    together
COGN, GNO—know
CONTRA—against
CORP—body
COSMO, COSM—world
CRAC, CRAT—rule, power
CRED—trust, believe
CRESC, CRET—grow
CULP—blame, fault
CURR, CURS—run
DE—down, out, apart
DEC—ten, tenth
DEMO, DEM—people

SAT VOCABULARY PREP LEVEL 1

DI, DIURN—day

DIA—across

DIC, DICT—speak

DIS, DIF, DI—not, apart, away

DOC, DOCT—teach

DOL—pain

DUC, DUCT—lead

EGO—self

EN, EM—in, into

ERR—wander

EU—well, good

EX, E—out, out of

FAC, FIC, FECT, FY, FEA—
	make, do

FAL, FALS—deceive

FERV—boil

FID—faith, trust

FLU, FLUX—flow

FORE—before

FRAG, FRAC—break

FUS—pour

GEN—birth, class, kin

GRAD, GRESS—step

GRAPH, GRAM—writing

GRAT—pleasing

GRAV, GRIEV—heavy

GREG—crowd, flock

HABIT, HIBIT—have, hold

HAP—by chance

HELIO, HELI—sun

HETERO—other

HOL—whole

HOMO—same

HOMO—man

HYDR—water

HYPER—too much, excess

HYPO—too little, under

IN, IG, IL, IM, IR—not

IN, IL, IM, IR—in, on, into

INTER—between, among

INTRA, INTR—within

IT, ITER—between, among

JECT, JET—throw

JOUR—day

JUD—judge

JUNCT, JUG—join

JUR—swear, law

LAT—side

LAV, LAU, LU—wash

LEG, LEC, LEX—read, speak

LEV—light

LIBER—free

LIG, LECT—choose, gather

LIG, LI, LY—bind

LING, LANG—tongue

LITER—letter

LITH—stone

LOQU, LOC, LOG—speech,
	thought

LUC, LUM—light

LUD, LUS—play

MACRO—great

MAG, MAJ, MAS, MAX—great

MAL—bad

MAN—hand

MAR—sea

MATER, MATR—mother

MEDI—middle

MEGA—great

MEM, MEN—remember

METER, METR, MENS—
    measure

MICRO—small

MIS—wrong, bad, hate

MIT, MISS—send

MOLL—soft

MON, MONIT—warn

MONO—one

MOR—custom, manner

MOR, MORT—dead

MORPH—shape

MOV, MOT, MOB, MOM—move

MUT—change

NAT, NASC—born

NAU, NAV—ship, sailor

NEG—not, deny

NEO—new

NIHIL—none, nothing

NOM, NYM—name

NOX, NIC, NEC, NOC—harm

NOV—new

NUMER—number

OB—against

OMNI—all

ONER—burden

OPER—work

PAC—peace

PALP—feel

PAN—all

PATER, PATR—father

PATH, PASS—feel, suffer

PEC—money

PED, POD—foot

PEL, PULS—drive

PEN—almost

PEND, PENS—hang

PER—through, by, for,
    throughout

PER—against, destruction

PERI—around

PET—seek, go towards

PHIL—love

PHOB—fear

PHON—sound

PLAC—calm, please

PON, POS—put, place

PORT—carry

POT—drink

POT—power

PRE—before

PRIM, PRI—first

PRO—ahead, forth

PROTO—first

PROX, PROP—near

SAT ROOT LIST

SAT VOCABULARY PREP

PSEUDO—false
PYR—fire
QUAD, QUAR, QUAT—four
QUES, QUER, QUIS, QUIR—
    question
QUIE—quiet
QUINT, QUIN—five
RADI, RAMI—branch
RECT, REG—straight, rule
REG—king, rule
RETRO—backward
RID, RIS—laugh
ROG—ask
RUD—rough, crude
RUPT—break
SACR, SANCT—holy
SCRIB, SCRIPT, SCRIV—write
SE—apart, away
SEC, SECT, SEG—cut
SED, SID—sit
SEM—seed, sow
SEN—old
SENT, SENS—feel, think
SEQU, SECU—follow
SIM, SEM—similar, same
SIGN—mark, sign
SIN—curve
SOL—sun
SOL—alone
SOMN—sleep
SON—sound

SOPH—wisdom
SPEC, SPIC—see, look
SPER—hope
SPERS, SPAR—scatter
SPIR—breathe
STRICT, STRING—bind
STRUCT, STRU—build
SUB—under
SUMM—highest
SUPER, SUR—above
SURGE, SURRECT—rise
SYN, SYM—together
TACIT, TIC—silent
TACT, TAG, TANG—touch
TEN, TIN, TAIN—hold, twist
TEND, TENS, TENT—stretch
TERM—end
TERR—earth, land
TEST—witness
THE—god
THERM—heat
TIM—fear, frightened
TOP—place
TORT—twist
TORP—stiff, numb
TOX—poison
TRACT—draw
TRANS—across, over,
    through, beyond
TREM, TREP—shake
TURB—shake

SAT ROOT LIST

UMBR—shadow

UNI, UN—one

URB—city

VAC—empty

VAL, VAIL—value, strength

VEN, VENT—come

VER—true

VERB—word

VERT, VERS—turn

VICT, VINC—conquer

VID, VIS—see

VIL—base, mean

VIV, VIT—life

VOC, VOK, VOW—call, voice

VOL—wish

VOLV, VOLUT—turn, roll

VOR—eat

SAT ROOT LIST